Praise For *50 Tax-Smart Investing Strategies* and Kurt Rosentreter

"Kurt Rosentreter has combined his excellent knowledge in the two fields of investments and tax to create **a unique reference** — one filled with powerful tax-saving strategies that are easy to implement . . . **a must read** for investors looking to keep more of what they earn!"

— ALAN PFAHL, CANADA TRUST TAX SERVICES

"*50 Tax-Smart Investing Stategies* . . . contains **all kinds of interesting ideas**, including tips on how to start building an RRSP for children under 18, ways to minimize tax on mutual funds, advice on how to manage registered and non-registered portfolios and a lot more."

— GORDON PAPE, *INTERNET WEALTH BUILDER #9812*

"*50 Tax-Smart Investing Stategies* is **a great reference book** and I enjoyed reading it."

— CAROL GAGNÉ, C.G.A.

"The first **credible** material I have been able to locate for reading on tax-smart investing."

— GREG OSTRANDER, LABOUR STANDARDS OFFICER, SASKATCHEWAN LABOUR

"It was **an eye-opener** . . . to realize how much easier it was to understand [mutual funds] with this book's clarifications."

— ANNE SMITH

"*50 Tax-Smart Investing Stategies* . . . is the first complete book I have come across which focuses specifically on investments and taxation, setting forth **useful and relevant** information in a **succinct and well-organized** manner . . . presenting the sometimes highly complex and technical data in a **readable and understandable** format."

— DONNA HOSSACK

50 TAX-SMART
INVESTING STRATEGIES

50 TAX-SMART INVESTING STRATEGIES

And Other Financial Tips to Maximize Your After-Tax Return and Net Worth

1999 Edition

Kurt Rosentreter, C.A.

This edition published in 1999 by Stoddart Publishing Co. Limited
34 Lesmill Road, Toronto, Canada M3B 2T6

First edition published in 1997 by Stoddart Publishing

Distributed in Canada by General Distribution Services Limited
325 Humber College Blvd., Toronto, Ontario M9W 7C3
Tel. (416) 213-1919   Fax (416) 213-1917
Email Customer.Service@ccmailgw.genpub.com

Canadian Cataloguing in Publication Data
Rosentreter, Kurt
50 tax-smart investing strategies: and other financial planning tips
to maximize your after-tax returns and net worth

Revised and updated.

ISBN 0-7737-6019-9

1. Tax planning — Canada — Popular works.
2. Finance, Personal — Canada.
I. Title.   II. Title: Fifty tax-smart investing strategies.

HG179.R678   1999   332.024   C98-932492-3

Cover design: Angel Guerra
Text design: Tannice Goddard
Typesetting: Kinetics Design & Illustration

Printed and bound in Canada

CONTENTS

Tax-Smart Investing Strategies: Other Investments

Other Tax-Smart Investing Strategies

Tax-Smart Investing Strategies for the Family

Tax-Smart RRSP/RRIF Strategies

Tax-Smart Insurance Strategies

Tax-Smart Strategies

Bonus Strategies:

PREFACE

All else being equal, if fund A returned 12.5% over the past 5 years, and fund B returned 11.8%, you'd buy fund A — right?

But consider that, after tax, fund A returned 10.5% and fund B returned 11.1%. Are you still choosing fund A? Probably not!

This focus on after-tax investing is long overdue.

As the next century approaches, all Canadians are trying to make their incomes go further as they fight rising costs of living, shrinking health-care coverage, and ever-increasing taxes. Separately, focusing on higher investment returns and lower taxes are effective ways to stretch incomes. But the combination of the two, called "*tax-smart investing*" or thinking about investing on an after-tax basis, can provide Canadians with a powerful tool for growing *net worth* and improving cash flow.

This book, by focusing on tax-smart investing, takes investing to a new level of thinking. Tax-smart investing means investing with taxes in mind *before* you buy. When you examine the Canadian marketplace for investment products, you will find many investment salespeople selling a broad array of investments, trying to produce the highest possible total return. Most investors, however, measure return on investment by the amount of money in their pockets at the end of the year as compared to the beginning of the year. This means *after-tax*. In this book, I will try to teach you to think more on an after-tax basis, and to educate you about investments and tax, and how to put them together effectively to maximize your after-tax returns.

As Canadians look to the financial marketplace for their investing needs, many are overwhelmed by the choice among thousands of investment products and thousands of people selling investments. This book feels for you as you succumb to investment- and financial-planning information overload in the Canadian marketplace today. This book will not tell you to "save for retirement." It will not cover the A-to-Zs of financial planning. This book provides 50 strategies designed to assist you in growing your net worth. To-the-point advice for busy Canadians who already have a basic understanding of personal finance.

The strategies presented here are not a comprehensive list, but rather serve as a starting point for examining how to maximize your personal net worth using a variety of techniques. Many of the strategies will require implementation assistance from an investment advisor, *financial planner*, or income tax specialist. Please consult a professional advisor for advice on how these strategies can be applied to your personal situation.

You should also bear in mind that the strategies in this book are based on an understanding of current and drafted income tax legislation. The Minister of Finance can make changes to the *Income Tax Act of Canada* at any time, and such changes could have a significant impact on these strategies and their applicability to your personal situation. A professional advisor will be able to determine the impact of any changes in tax legislation that occur after the publishing of this book, and should be consulted to determine the applicability of these strategies to your personal situation.

Each of the following 50 strategies is coupled with an example to illustrate the investment techniques being discussed. You can also follow along in many of the strategies as I "crunch the numbers" to give you a sense of the real savings that can be achieved with tax-smart investing. For the sake of simplicity, I make one or two basic assumptions with the calculations: a rate of 50% is used to represent taxation of regular income in the highest tax bracket in Canada; and unless otherwise stated, dividends are Canadian-sourced dividends that qualify for tax-advantaged treatment in Canada when taxed in an individual's hands.

I have also included a glossary of financial terms to help you as you read these strategies. If you see a word or phrase in italics and are not sure what the term means, you can look it up at the back of the book.

Finally, you will notice that I have deliberately avoided referring to real financial products and companies in this book. Here's why. There are many good investment and insurance products sold and serviced by many highly qualified professional advisors in Canada. But you will have specific needs, which should be served by specific solutions. It would be misleading for me to suggest that one particular product fits everyone's personal situation. Instead, I have chosen to provide concepts and strategies around which products can be added.

Take the concepts described in these strategies and, alone or with your financial advisor, seek the product solutions in the marketplace that apply these concepts and address your financial needs and objectives. I hope that you achieve the same value from these strategies that many of my clients already have.

INTRODUCTION

What Is Tax-Smart Investing?

Tax-smart investing is investing to maximize the after-tax return on investments. It means maximizing what you earn, after paying income taxes.

Achieving the after-tax rate of return you desire when you invest is a function of two related factors: buying an investment product that achieves a certain total rate of return; and paying the income tax on the total return earned by the investment product. Many investors and advisors focus only on the investment product when they invest, and neglect to consider the tax impact on their total rate of return. Remember, the *interest* income, *dividends,* and *capital gains* that you include on your tax return, and the tax you pay on this income, affect your rates of return on your taxable investments. The tax paid on this investment income reduces the overall return or profitability of an investment product.

You need to look at the total picture, including taxation, to understand how well your investments are doing. Failure to consider the tax effects of investing may result in misleading returns and missed financial goals, as a large slice of tax may be taken from the total returns earned.

Tax-smart investing is about minimizing and/or deferring the income tax paid on investment earnings in order to maximize after-tax returns. And tax-smart investing is about implementing other tax-smart strategies across your financial needs spectrum, integrating all areas of *financial planning* to maximize your total personal net worth.

Over any individual's lifetime, there is probably no greater expenditure made than taxes. Given this, it is in everyone's best interest to implement as many tax-saving and tax-deferral strategies as possible.

To utilize tax-smart investing strategies, investors and their advisors must understand the taxation of the different investment products available today. Additionally, investors and their advisors should understand the investor's *marginal tax rate*, and marginal tax rate of the investor's spouse and children.

Tax: Only Part of Proper Investment Planning

Tax-smart strategies should be contemplated in the context of your overall investment strategy. The tax effectiveness of investing is only one factor to consider when investing, and investing should not be contemplated for tax reasons alone. Other factors to consider when investing include, but are not limited to, investment performance expectations and needs, investor *risk tolerance*, investment *diversification*, current investment holdings, and *liquidity* needs.

Investors should consult their own professional financial advisors before implementing any of the strategies that follow. The applicability of these 50 strategies to any individual will depend on that individual's personal situation, including tax, financial, legal, and investment characteristics. Investors and their advisors should also evaluate the impact of future changes to the *Income Tax Act* and other statutes and the impact of these changes to their planning strategies.

The Mistake of Trying to Manage Your Own Money

Most people aren't in the habit of fixing their own cars, prescribing their own medicine, or even booking their own vacations. Yet so many individuals think that they can do their own investing.

Investing today is more than a full-time job for a professional advisor. There are now over 2,000 *mutual funds*, hundreds of different *stocks* and *bonds*, dozens of countries to consider investing in, and all kinds of specialty products. If you hold down a full-time job, and have a personal life, when do you have time to keep up to date on thousands of investments?

But investing is more than that . . . you must understand tax laws, investment theory, economics, and monetary policy in Canada and beyond. Investment professionals have years of academic training to go along with years of experience. It is unrealistic to think you can learn enough in your spare time to do better than they can over the long term.

And that's really what we are talking about — doing better than professional *money managers* or investment advisors. You may outperform the pros now and then, but it may be almost impossible to do it consistently over time. With that said, let's examine the general types of advisors that exist in the marketplace. Use these descriptions to sort out what is best for your needs.

- Financial Planner — A professional advisor who is qualified to advise you on matters of retirement, debts, estate, taxes, investing, and other basic personal finance topics. The *CFP* (Certified Financial Planner) designation is the industry standard, and use of this title is regulated by the Financial Planning Standards of Canada. Beware an advisor called simply a "*financial planner*" in Canada (using the title "financial planner" is currently unregulated in Canada and consumers should ensure their advisors are highly qualified and experienced). Having the CFP designation, among others, is a good start.

A financial planner is like a general practitioner in medicine — an advisor with a basic understanding of many issues, but a specialist in few. When you have complex matters, search out a specialist or at least get a second opinion.

- Financial Advisor at a full-service brokerage (aka "broker", or "*portfolio* manager") — A *brokerage* advisor will understand a client's personal circumstances and build an investment portfolio around that client's needs. The advisor provides ongoing client service, including advice on what to buy and sell, and can provide a choice of investments from a variety of suppliers. Using a *full-service advisor* can mean you are purchasing a top level service, often accompanied by the highest fees.

  Investigate the qualifications and experience of full-service advisors: stay away from advisors who are no more than sales people for investment products. Look for qualifications like "FCSI" and "CFA," financial degrees from universities, and relevant experience. Also realize that these advisors are paid based on the products they sell you, and you should be comfortable with this perceived lack of objectivity. For the level of fees you pay at a full-service brokerage (fees you don't always see), you should question the value you get.

- Discount Brokerage Services — *Discount brokerages* offer access to the same wide range of products available through a full-service brokerage, but there is no advisor attached to provide advice on what to buy. Without an advisor, you must rely on the Internet, newsletters, your own research, and newspapers. Fees are typically lower for discount brokerage services. The discount *broker* will simply execute orders, not offer any advice.

- Account Representative for a Money Manager — If you invest directly with a professional money manager firm (like a mutual *fund company*), you may be assigned an account representative who assists you in selecting investments (the money manager's investments only), reviews *performance* with you, and re-balances your investments regularly. These individuals do not select investments owned inside the funds, but rather they serve as a bridge between you and the professional money managers who do manage the funds. In this way, the money managers are not usually distracted by marketing, client service, or administrative responsibilities, and can focus on making you money.
- Mutual Fund Agent — Many advisors, financial planners, and insurance agents are licensed to sell mutual funds only.

Worth Noting

Beware investment advisors who hold themselves out to be *estate* planners, tax advisors, *life insurance* agents, and financial planners, all at once. It is more than a full-time job to be just an investment advisor. Be careful with someone who is trying to be everything to everyone.

Determine which type(s) of advice you require, then comparison shop.

STRATEGY #1

The Starting Point:
Know Your Marginal Tax Rate

Your *marginal tax rate* is the tax rate applicable to the next dollar of *taxable income* you earn. The Canadian tax system uses progressive tax rates, whereby the rate of tax increases as taxable income increases, up to a certain point. Marginal rates of tax vary according to province or territory of residence in Canada, and according to type of income. Understanding marginal tax rates can help you to understand tax paid on incremental income and how that tax may differ according to the nature of the income.

Knowing your own marginal tax rate is important in order to plan how to minimize the tax you pay on additional income. Also, knowing the marginal tax rates of different income types permits you to reduce taxes paid, by varying your investment mix.

Understanding Taxation of Income Types

Different types of income attract different levels of taxation. Therefore, one of your considerations when buying investments should be the amount of taxes you are going to pay on the type of income earned. The types of income you can earn include *regular income* from business, employment, pension, and retirement; and *investment income*, including *interest*, rent, *dividends*, and *capital gains.* Regular income, along with interest income, is the most highly taxed income type. Interest income is earned from bank accounts and from fixed income investments like Canada Savings Bonds, *guaranteed investment certificates* (GICs), and government *Treasury bills.*

Dividends are *distributions* of after-tax income paid by *corporations* to their shareholders. You may receive dividends from the *mutual funds* you own, if the funds own *shares* of corporations that pay dividends. Canadian dividends (or simply "dividends") generally attract the least amount of tax among all income types.

Capital gains result when you sell an asset for more than its purchase price. The increase in value is a capital gain, and 75% of the gain (called a *taxable capital gain*) is included in your personal income for tax purposes. Capital gains generally attract more tax than dividends but less than interest and regular income. There are two types of capital gains: realized and unrealized. An *unrealized gain* consists of the *accrued capital gain* on an *asset* before the asset is sold or deemed to be sold. A realized gain generally results when the asset is sold or deemed to be sold.

Note that interest income earned is usually taxable annually, whether it is received or not. Dividends are generally taxed when received. Capital gains, however, are taxable only when realized; that means you may be able to own an investment that has a growing market value and not trigger any tax until it is sold.

Why Knowing Your Marginal Tax Rate Is Important

Knowing your marginal tax rate permits you to calculate the *after-tax rate of return* on additional investment income. It also permits you to calculate the tax savings on your *registered retirement savings plan* (RRSP) deductions. This knowledge may affect the way you decide to invest your money. Since we all care about what is left in our pockets after-tax, having an understanding of the rates is important to us all.

Below I have approximated the marginal tax rates for different taxable income levels in Canada (combined federal and provincial rates). Keep in mind that each province has its own exact rate, which differs from those presented here. For our purposes, however, these approximations are reasonable.

Taxable Income Level	Interest & Regular Income	Dividends	Capital Gains
$6,457 to $29,590	27%	8%	20%
$29,591 to $59,180	43%	27%	32%
$59,181 to $62,195	48%	32%	36%
Greater than $62,195	50%	34%	38%

Here is an approximation of the marginal tax rates on different types of income for someone with taxable income of $30,000 a year:

An additional $1 of interest or regular income would be taxed at a rate of 43%.

An additional $1 of dividend income would be taxed at a rate of 27%.

An additional $1 of capital gains would be taxed at a rate of 32%.

For an individual with a taxable income of $70,000 a year or more,

An additional $1 of interest or regular income would be taxed at a rate of 50%.

An additional $1 of dividend income would be taxed at a rate of 34%.

An additional $1 of capital gains would be taxed at a rate of 38%.

▼

Example

Rieva earned $33,000 of taxable income in 1998. She hopes to climb the company ladder quickly and anticipates that her salary will rise rapidly. When it came time to make her *RRSP contribution* for 1998, Rieva wanted the most bang for her RRSP buck. She reviewed her marginal tax rate and income level, and learned that she had just moved into a higher tax bracket by approximately $3,500 ($33,000 taxable income less $29,500 taxable income threshold from the above table). According to the above marginal income tax rate chart, on this last $3,500 of income she would be taxed at 43% instead of 27%.

Rieva decided to make an RRSP contribution for $4,000 but only take the tax deduction for $3,500. (We all have the ability to make a contribution but delay taking the corresponding deduction.) This strategy accomplished several things. First, the RRSP deduction reduced her taxable income to $29,500, eliminating the need for her to pay the more expensive tax that year at the 43% level, and improving her cash flow. Second, she tax-sheltered as much investable wealth as she could, growing her RRSP and deferring tax on investment income until a future withdrawal from her RRSP. Third, she carried forward $500 of unused deduction to future years and can apply it against future *higher-tax-rate income*, generating more tax refund for her RRSP dollars. Rieva can continue to selectively apply her RRSP deductions when she chooses in order to minimize paying tax at the higher tax brackets.

Delaying taking a deduction this year can be a good strategy if the future tax benefit outweighs the opportunity cost given up by not taking the deduction this year to get a larger tax refund now and more tax-sheltered growth. For Rieva, knowing her marginal tax rate permits her to "fine-tune" her RRSP strategies to maximize her deduction value — and minimize tax paid.

▼

Bonus Tip

Determining your spouse's marginal tax rate will help to determine who should save and who should pay expenses in the family. The lower earner should be the one saving (outside RRSPs), since less tax will be payable if the lower earner is generating investment income.

STRATEGY #2

Avoid Year-End Mutual Fund Purchases

All year long, *mutual funds* may provide *unit holders* with investment income. They may also increase in value as the fund investments appreciate. This appreciation will provide *unit* holders with a *capital gain* on the eventual sale of the fund units. Both the income and the appreciation of investments accumulate inside the fund, and they are reflected through an increasing fund price.

Monthly, quarterly, or at year end, funds may make *distributions* (of the income or gains earned inside the fund) to the unit holders. The nature of a mutual fund trust is such that certain types of income earned by the investments owned by the trust — *dividends* or capital gains — retain their identity when distributed to individuals. These distributions reduce the value of fund units by the amount of the distributions per unit. Unit holders receiving distributions will have to pay tax on the distributions if the mutual fund is owned outside an *RRSP* or *RRIF*.

Because of the year-end process described above, if you purchase mutual funds late in the year you may pay an increased fund price (reflecting the accumulated income inside the fund), and then witness a reduction of this price on (perhaps) December 31, when a distribution is paid to you as a unit holder. This can also occur more often, if distributions are made quarterly, semi-annually, or monthly.

As a new fund buyer, you have paid for the income and gains that may have accrued inside the fund all year long, even though you didn't earn them. The result is that you are prepaying tax on future increases in value. These distributions will be taxed at your *marginal tax rate* if this investment is held outside an RRSP or RRIF.

Worse still, someone who purchases the same fund early in the following year (after distributions are made), at a reduced price (because of the distributions), doesn't have to pay any tax because he or she didn't receive any distributions from the previous year. He or she is currently ahead of you by the amount of tax you will have to pay in April, simply because of the timing of the purchase.

You could have avoided this tax pitfall by waiting until after the distribution was made to make your purchase — on January 1 or later of the next year. But bear in mind that some will argue that waiting until the next year may cost you more in lost return than you will save in tax. This may occur, so you need to balance the risk of lost return with the disadvantage of paying additional tax.

Bonus Tip

If the investor purchasing the fund is not taxable (for example, if you purchase a growth mutual fund for a child who has no other income), a *taxable capital gains* distribution of approximately $7,000 to the child each year can be received tax free, as the income will be offset by the child's personal *tax credit*.

The distribution will be added to the *adjusted cost base* of the fund, which will also help to reduce any future capital gain and resulting tax on the sale of the fund.

▼

Example

Tom purchased 100 units of XY mutual fund late in December 1998 for $5,000 or $50 per unit. On December 31, 1998, XY mutual fund paid Tom a distribution of $5 per unit, which was reinvested in the fund to buy approximately 11 more units ($500 of income/$45; when Tom was paid this distribution by the fund, the fund unit market price dropped to $45 per unit). The distribution was *regular income*, according to the *T3 slip* Tom received early in the new year from the *fund company*.

Tom had to pay 50% tax on the $500 of distributions, since he was in the top marginal tax bracket in his province. In total, Tom now had 111 units worth $5,000; the same value as before, but he also had to pay tax of 50% x $500 on distributions, or $250. His investment was worth $5,000, but cost him $5,250.

Sharon, Tom's wife, made exactly the same purchase only days later, in January 1999. She paid $45 per unit for 111 units, for a total of approximately $5,000. But she had no additional tax to pay, because she was receiving no income from the funds for the previous year. Sharon was ahead of Tom by $250 strictly because of the timing of the purchase.

So consider waiting until the new year when buying those year-end bargains! They may not be the bargains you think they are.

STRATEGY #3

Invest in Growth Investments Outside Your RRSP/RRIF

The growth investments we are talking about here are *equity mutual funds*. These funds generally invest in *common shares* of *public corporations*. An equity mutual fund might, for example, own *stock* of the XYZ Bank of Canada. This stock may regularly pay *dividends* to the fund, which may be then distributed to you as the *unit holder*. Additionally, when the *fund manager* sells the stock inside the fund and buys stock of another corporation, there may be a *capital gain* on the sale of the *shares*. Again, this capital gain may be distributed to you.

Many equity mutual funds distribute at least some dividends, capital gains, and even *interest* income annually. If you hold these investments outside your *RRSP* or *RRIF*, you pay tax on these *distributions*, even if the funds are automatically reinvested in more fund *units*. This may not be a desirable scenario — paying tax on income and gains you don't even get (because they are reinvested). This income is reported on those *T3 slips* you get at tax time every spring.

However, some mutual funds are more "*tax smart*." These are mutual funds that do not make significant distributions to investors each year. How do they do this? By purchasing shares in companies focused on growth of their business rather than on generating income to shareholders through dividend payments — stocks with increasing share price, resulting in part from reinvestment of earnings they might otherwise have paid out as dividends to shareholders. These companies use the money to grow, hire employees, upgrade systems, etc. A mutual fund holding such "growth" companies should not generate much regular income since the fund investments are not generating any. Instead, your return is composed of increasing value of the stocks owned by the fund, a value that isn't taxable until the stock is disposed of by the fund manager or you sell your fund units. In other words, taxation of your return is deferred!

Fund managers can also minimize taxable distributions by selling investments inside the mutual fund less frequently. (See Strategy #25 on the benefits of a *buy-and-hold* strategy.) Sales trigger the realization of any *accrued capital gains* that might exist on a stock investment made by the fund. Holding on to the stock longer defers the *realization of the gain* that would be allocated to you as a unit holder, and thus you can also defer the payment of tax.

Be on the lookout for fund managers who trade heavily and/or hold large *cash positions*. Heavy trading may generate large amounts of *taxable capital gains*, which are distributed to you and are taxable in your hands. Cash levels inside a fund may produce interest income that is taxable to you at the highest tax rates applicable to investment income. Note that fund managers may not pay much attention to tax-smart investing since showing the highest *pre-tax return* is generally what they are ranked and rewarded on.

Overall, if you can find a fund that doesn't buy and sell heavily each year and also invests in stocks paying little or no distributions, you may be able to create an RRSP effect outside of your RRSP but without the *tax deduction*. Without

selling investments or receiving income from those investments, you may be able to earn pure *tax-deferred growth* from
the rising value of the mutual fund. As we learned earlier,
accruing capital gains are not taxed until the related investment is disposed of. However, be cautious in selecting these
investments. Remember, as a mutual fund unit holder, you
cannot control when the fund manager sells the investments
the fund owns.

▼

Example

Heather has been renting her home for a long time, and is
interested in purchasing some equity mutual funds for saving purposes in order to buy a condominium for retirement
in eight years' time. She had her investment advisor provide
her with a list of three equity funds that had paid little or no
distributions recently:

- ABC Canadian Equity Fund: good returns last three
  years; *MER* of 2.8%; distributed $0.10 of dividends, $0.10
  of capital gains, and $0.05 of interest per unit to unit
  holders last year.
- DEF Canadian Growth Fund: good returns last three
  years; MER of 2.25%; no distributions last year.
- GHI Canadian Fund: good returns last three years; MER
  of 1.5%; distributed $0.30 of dividends per unit to unit
  holders last year.

Heather decided on the DEF mutual fund, because it has
paid no distributions in the last three years and has seen a
significant increase in unit value from appreciation in the
share prices of the underlying investments. The fund manager's style is one of "value," meaning that he tries to buy
stocks that are *undervalued* and then hold them for the long

term for capital appreciation ("buy-and-hold" strategy). This means there shouldn't be much stock-selling each year by the fund manager. Owning this fund will allow Heather to accumulate savings through deferred growth on the fund, which will be taxable only when the fund is sold. Of course, there may be some taxable distributions, particularly when sales are required to fund large redemptions. But most distributions hopefully will be minimized through Heather's fund selection and understanding of fund management policies ("buy-hold" style).

Heather's investment advisor pointed out that the same strategy could be implemented in another way, with a bit more control for Heather. She could purchase a stock — not a fund — that doesn't pay any dividends, and hold the stock until a point in the future. Since she owns the stock directly, she controls all buy-and-sell decisions. No tax would result until the stock is sold and a capital gain is realized. (Unfortunately, the trade-off when buying stocks directly is that you may not have enough money to create a broadly diversified *portfolio* and will have higher investment risk as a result.)

The investment advisor also pointed out one other interesting point: sometimes a mutual fund appears to produce little or no distributions annually and therefore seems quite tax efficient. Upon closer examination of the DEF fund, however, you may notice that the fund actually does earn dividend and interest income but this income is eaten up by management expenses charged against the fund by the *fund company*. When this happens, the income seems to disappear like it never existed, and there are no distributions. The investment advisor advised Heather not to be fooled by these types of funds where a high management expense ratio (MER) offsets the distributions, making it appear tax efficient. A lower MER and some distributions is usually better than high expenses where you get nothing at all. With some distributions, even after-tax, you are at least left with something in your pocket.

STRATEGY #4

Purchase Mutual Funds Holding Small Accrued Gains

This is a hard strategy to implement, because everyone wants to own successful *mutual funds*. Unfortunately, many of us tend to jump in after the fund has already been successful for a while. This is not always a smart move. Here's why. A successful *equity mutual fund* is one in which the *fund manager* purchased *stocks* that have since increased in value. This increase in stock value inside the fund means the value of the mutual fund has increased and the fund is holding several stock investments with *accrued capital gains*. Now you come along and want to buy the fund.

What happens when you buy a successful equity fund that is holding many stocks that have already increased in value? You are buying a fund that is holding accrued capital gains you didn't earn, yet on which you will be paying tax. If the fund sells those stocks tomorrow, the tax liability arising from the sale of those stocks is distributed to you (and other *unit holders*) in the form of a *taxable capital gain*. At tax time, you will pay tax on gains you may not have earned but received as a *distribution*. Of course, this matters only for funds owned outside an *RRSP* or *RRIF*. Also, this tax issue is more of a concern with funds that practise *buy-and-hold* policies than with funds that buy and sell often. Funds that buy and sell stocks frequently may not hold investments long enough to accumulate large accrued gains. The drawback is that the frequent selling by the fund manager does result in more frequent taxation of capital gains, which may be undesirable to existing unit holders.

One way to minimize the chance of buying a fund with significant accrued tax liabilities is to purchase a brand-new mutual fund when it first becomes available. In this case, the mutual fund likely has just recently purchased many of the investments it holds, and accrued capital gains may be small.

Another option is to purchase equity funds inside your RRSP or RRIF, where taxation of income and capital gains is not an issue. This option, however, does not let you enjoy the lower taxation of *tax-advantaged* capital gains earned from stocks and equity funds held outside an RRSP or RRIF.

Tax-smart investing suggests that *equities* should be a part of every balanced RRSP/RRIF and non-RRSP/RRIF *portfolio*. But be aware of the existence of potential accrued tax liabilities when purchasing equity funds with large accrued capital gains buried in their portfolio. If you want to buy a "*hot*" *fund*, watch for funds that are "*capped*" or closed off to new investment, and then watch for the *fund company* to replicate the old fund — that is, create a similar fund. That may be a better time to buy: when the tax base on the investments is fresh and no significant capital gains yet exist.

Yet another way to avoid these hidden tax liabilities is to move out of mutual funds and *pooled funds* completely, and utilize *segregated money management* through a *money manager*, or through a segregated *wrapped product*. These products use your money to purchase a new portfolio of stocks and *bonds* such that the tax you pay on accrued capital gains is directly attributable to your market successes. For more information, see Strategy #18 on segregated wrapped products.

A final tip: when you do intend to buy a replicated fund, investigate just how similar it is. Mutual fund companies in Canada have produced some "*clone*" funds that have higher fees. If this is the case, you may want to compare the long-term profitability of the new fund with its small existing accrued capital gains versus a less expensive fund with larger accrued capital gains.

▼

Example

Peter just received $15,000 from the sale of stock he inherited 10 years ago. His cost base was only $1,000. He realizes that he will have to pay tax on the capital gain next year, so he has put $3,000 in a GIC to cover the expected tax bill (based on his calculation of tax using his *marginal tax rate*). The other $12,000 he wants to invest long-term outside his RRSP in a good-quality Canadian equity mutual fund.

After some research, Peter found what he thought was a superb mutual fund, which had just produced a 50% return over the last two years. Newspapers reported that investors were contributing millions of dollars of new money to the fund each week. Peter decided this was the fund to buy, but he wanted a second opinion from his investment advisor.

After the advisor assessed Peter's objectives, needs, and *risk tolerance*, she confirmed that Peter's pick made sense. The advisor also told Peter to wait a month, because the fund was about to be "capped" or closed off to new investment due to its phenomenal growth. The advisor said that the fund company was going to create a new fund that would be a clone of the first.

For Peter and all investors, there can be significant tax

15

advantages in buying the new clone fund instead of the old one. While the two funds contain similar investments, the tax impact on new investors may be quite different. In the old fund, investments that have done well over the last two years may have large accrued capital gains, which will be distributed to fund unit holders when the stock is eventually sold inside the fund. As mentioned before, in this case a new investor may be allocated a large taxable gain that he or she hasn't earned, but has inherited when the fund was bought, and will have to pay the related tax on. If the investor buys the new mutual fund instead, he or she can buy virtually the same investments but without the built-in tax liability. Since all the stock investments will be recent purchases in the new fund, new investors will be taxed on whatever gains they earn. However, the longer they wait to buy the new fund, the more likely they are to run into the same problem — so it is important to buy early.

STRATEGY #5

Don't Rush to Buy Mutual Funds on a Deferred-Load Basis

Did you know that when you bought your last *mutual fund* investment for your *RRSP* or *RRIF* and chose the *deferred-load* fee option (deferred service charge) instead of paying a *front-end-load* fee, you may have chosen the more expensive fee option?

Mutual funds are often sold with no upfront fee to you but with a declining deferred-load fee which you will potentially never pay — if you hold the fund long enough. Inside your RRSP, where you are usually investing for 10 years or more, this sounds great. But it may not be. There is another set of expenses that all mutual fund owners pay annually. Inside the mutual fund, the *fund company* charges the fund administrative expenses, operating expenses, and management fees to maintain the fund. These fees are deducted from the fund's annual gross return to produce the net rate of return you get. These internal fees are collectively called *management expenses*, and are expressed in the form of a *management expense ratio* (MER).

Understanding how these internal fees work is important,

because some fund companies offer two or more similar mutual funds with different fee options. In such cases, the internal fees can also vary widely from fund to fund. For example, if you buy fund X on a deferred-load basis, the internal management fees for this fund may be 2.5% each year. You may never know about the internal fees if you tend to focus on the net return to you after these fees are deducted (that's how the returns are shown in the newspapers). However, the fund company may also offer another fund (with similar investment holdings to those of fund X) that is being sold with a *front-end-load* fee of 2% but an internal fee of only 2.25%. While the idea of paying a 2% upfront fee may not appear attractive to you, and it's an easier sell for your investment advisor to sell you a fund with no upfront fee, over several years you may be earning less with the deferred-load fund, because of the reduced net return due to its higher annual internal fees.

To determine which is the least expensive alternative for you, ask your advisor (1) to tell you if the funds you are considering buying have multiple expense options for similar funds, and (2) to calculate which option is less costly to you depending on your needs. Evaluate these considerations alongside the advisor's first responsibility — to make you money!

▼

Example

Calvin had been relying on his mutual fund agent to sell him the right funds for his RRSP. He hadn't given much thought to the funds the agent recommended, but had assumed the agent had researched the picks and what he was buying was the best. That's why Calvin was surprised recently when he attended a *financial planning* meeting with an advisor, set up by Calvin's employer. When the advisor reviewed Calvin's mutual fund holdings, he told Calvin that with some of his mutual fund holdings, his agent had selected the more expensive fee option where there were two fee options. Calvin had thought that by paying on a deferred-load basis he had chosen the cheaper way to buy. The advisor explained that buying on a deferred-load basis avoided only the purchase *commission* on the buying of a fund. But the funds in question had a higher internal expense ratio (MER) than the similar front-end-load funds offered by the same fund company. Depending how long Calvin plans to own the funds, he may pay more through internal fund expenses than any one-time load would ever cost.

Additionally, the advisor noted that one of the deferred-load funds that Calvin bought attributed much of its past success to a *star manager* who recently left the fund to join a competitor. The fund company had replaced the star with a relatively unproven manager. Since Calvin has been encouraged to hold long-term because he bought on a deferred-load basis, unless he sells and pays the deferred load, he doesn't get the benefit of a fund managed by the successful manager who had attracted him in the first place.

Calvin's advisor told him that before he purchases any funds he should inquire if the particular fund has a sister fund with a different fee structure. If there are sister funds with different MERs, he should consider having his advisor evaluate which will be the least expensive option during the planned holding period.

Crunching the Numbers

What Calvin bought: he paid $1,000 for a mutual fund with an internal MER of 2.25%. He bought on a deferred-load basis so there were no purchasing fees. Instead, the deferred load declined to zero after seven years.

At the end of 20 years, assuming an 8% growth rate less

the 2.25% MER, full reinvestment of income, and that these investments have been held inside an RRSP, the fund Calvin bought will be worth approximately $3,000.

What Calvin could have bought: he could have paid $1,000 for a sister fund that includes a 2% front-end-load fee. The fee will be $20, and the net investment amount will be $980. However, this fund has an internal MER of only 2%.

Under the same assumptions, the fund Calvin could have bought would be worth approximately $3,100 in 20 years. While the difference appears small here, keep in mind that on $100,000 (instead of $1,000), this difference is almost $10,000.

STRATEGY #6

Invest in Some Index Funds

Index mutual funds are investment products that attempt to mirror the *performance* of recognized capital market indices. These *mutual funds* may purchase the same *stocks* in the same proportions that exist inside a particular *index*, or they may purchase *derivatives* that lock in the change of an index (see Strategy #7). Indices like the *TSE 300* in Canada and the S&P 500 in the United States are examples of indices mutual funds have attempted to mirror. *Bond* market indices are also commonly replicated, primarily tracking the Scotia Capital Markets Universe Bond Index in Canada. *Equity* indices may consist of the largest companies in their respective countries. Some indices include companies that are representative of industries and the economy of the country in general. Other indices are more industry or country specific.

A mutual fund that attempts to mirror an index by purchasing similar stock and bond holdings tries to have similar performance as the index less a fee to the *fund company* to manage the fund and pay the operating costs. *Performance* may also differ slightly if the fund company doesn't buy and sell

shares of stock at the same time the index changes the companies in the index, a difference generally referred to as *tracking
error*. Generally, however, the performance of an index mutual
fund should be very similar to the actual index, less fees.

For tax-smart investors, index funds can be attractive. There
are several reasons to consider purchasing index funds:

* Index funds that mirror the TSE 300 or S&P 500 consist
  of investments that generally are the largest and some of
  the most successful companies in Canada and the U.S.
  respectively. Owning the investments included in these
  indices serves to diversify your money across industries
  and countries, and this reduces the risk of a significant
  loss occurring because of a loss in one particular region
  or industry sector.
* Indices like the TSE 300 traditionally have had low
  turnover of stocks. This translates to an index fund that
  holds most of its *portfolio* year after year (a form of *buy-
  and-hold*), and deferral of taxation of gains. This differs
  from a fund that buys and sells frequently, potentially
  realizing *taxable capital gains* with each sale.
* Index funds are usually fully invested. This means that
  the funds have little or no cash balances earning a low
  rate of return. Also, the interest income generated by
  cash balances is *tax disadvantaged* because of the high
  tax rate applied to it. Index funds may have little or no
  interest income, depending on the nature of the funds,
  increasing the potential to earn tax-advantaged *dividends*
  and *capital gains*. In successful markets where stock prices
  are rising, holding cash can be a disadvantage, while in
  down markets holding cash can reduce losses.
* Over the long term, index funds have outperformed many
  actively managed funds in the U.S. and Canada. While
  many funds now and then will outperform an index fund,
  far fewer can do it consistently over time. Ask your invest-

ment advisor to compare your Canadian equity funds to the TSE 300 over the last five years and see if the active management has outperformed a passively managed index with no manager.

• Index funds usually have lower *MERs* than their actively managed counterparts. Without salaries to pay for managers and no need to fly to (say) Brazil to research new investments, the cost of running the funds can be a lot less. Unfortunately, however, in many cases index funds are low cost because they pay no *commissions* or *trailer fees* to *brokers* or advisors and, sadly, may not be recommended to clients because of this.

• With index funds, understanding how well you are doing is easier. If you own an index fund that tracks the TSE 300, you can usually find the return for the TSE 300 in most Canadian newspapers, and this should approximate your fund's rate of return (less fees). If you own an actively managed fund, you have to search a little harder to find out how well you are doing.

▼

Example

Shannon usually picks current *hot funds* for her new *RRSP* investments. These are funds that everyone is buying, usually because of outstanding performance resulting from good active management. This year Shannon's investment advisor introduced her to index mutual funds and suggested she consider some of these funds for a piece of her investment portfolio. Shannon was initially sceptical — she is attracted by the potential of big returns — but the investment advisor demonstrated how many active funds do not beat the index funds, yet these active funds in some cases charge three times as much in MERs. Talk about paying more to underperform!

Shannon started to like the idea of owning some index mutual funds. She decided to invest in index funds because she liked the possibility of building a strong core of blue-chip index funds around which she could add active managers. She had her investment advisor set up a monthly purchase of an index fund that mirrored the TSE 300 for her Canadian content. She also had her advisor set up a monthly purchase of a U.S. equity mutual fund that mirrored the S&P 500. (The U.S. component was limited to her permissible 20% *foreign content* limit.)

Shannon is now committed to owning some index mutual funds. She knows that her index funds are invested in North America's biggest companies, which is less risky than the way some of her other funds are invested. She likes not having to worry about her favourite money manager leaving the current hot fund, since index funds have no active managers. She likes that the fund management is minimal (because index funds are designed only to match the broadly recognized index) and therefore the fund company charges much lower fees compared to the fees of equity funds that require *active management.*

Shannon was also impressed with the long-term historical returns for her two index funds. In many cases they exceed the returns of many actively managed funds investing in Canada and the U.S. And when she factored in the loads of actively managed funds, their higher MERs, and the taxation that results when funds buy and sell frequently, index funds became even more attractive.

Shannon admits she still wants to buy some hot funds and some other actively managed funds that she thinks can beat the market indices routinely. However, she is committed to adding these types of funds as "flavour" around her core holding of index funds.

STRATEGY #7

Know When to Buy Natural Versus Synthetic Index Funds

I have already encouraged you to examine investing in *index mutual funds* (see Strategy #6). Now let's fine-tune that strategy. Buy *natural index funds* outside an *RRSP* or *RRIF* and buy *synthetic index funds* inside an RRSP or RRIF.

Natural index funds are funds that replicate an index by purchasing the underlying investments that compose the index. For a Canadian equity index fund, for example, the *fund manager* might purchase the *stock* of corporations included in the *TSE 300* in the same proportion reflected in the index. Synthetic index funds are funds that may use *derivatives* to purchase exposure to a particular index. Synthetic funds are more fully described in Strategy #39. A synthetic fund may use a *futures* contract to provide investors with a rate of return equal to the change in the index, rather than buying actual stocks.

While these two types of index funds appear to be similar, they can be very different for tax purposes. Generally, *distributions* from synthetic index funds are taxed as ordinary income in Canada because they earn *interest* income from *Treasury bill* investments and ordinary income from derivatives. Some index fund managers have concluded that the distributions from the derivatives are more appropriately treated as *capital gains.* Keep in mind, however, that if you take this position in your tax return (treating the distributions as capital gains), you may be challenged by Revenue Canada.

Since natural index funds hold investments in real companies, they are *tax advantaged* compared to synthetic funds holding derivatives. Natural funds can flow out to *unit holders* the *dividends* paid by the funds' corporate investments. They can also flow out capital gains earned on the sale of stock. These dividends and capital gains are tax advantaged in Canada.

What does this all mean? It means that *tax-smart* investing indicates you should invest in natural index funds outside your RRSP or RRIF, where tax effectiveness matters, and invest in synthetic index funds inside your RRSP or RRIF, where tax is less important.

How can you tell whether an index fund is synthetic or not? Look at the fund holdings as provided by your investment advisor. If the holdings consist of *shares* in companies, you have found a natural index fund. If the holdings are Treasury bills and some futures contracts, you have likely found a synthetic index fund. Alternatively, ask your investment advisor to determine which funds are natural and which are synthetic.

▼

Example

Lana is a believer in index fund investing and already holds some global index funds inside her RRSP. She recently received a cash gift from her grandmother and decided to invest this money as a long-term investment outside her RRSP. She wanted to investigate more equity index funds, so she turned to her financial advisor for help. Because the financial advisor had sold Lana her other index funds, she knew Lana was already knowledgeable about the characteristics of the investment. But because the previous purchase was inside the RRSP, the advisor hadn't explained the tax effects of different types of index funds. Now appeared to be the right time.

Lana is currently in the highest tax bracket in Canada and is taxed at approximately 50% on all new *regular income*. Another index fund investment would provide new income, so the financial advisor explained to Lana how she should strive to obtain some dividends from her index funds in order to obtain favourable tax treatment. The advisor explained how synthetic index funds may distribute only regular income, which would be taxed at a higher rate than dividends or capital gains. A similar investment, but the potential for a much different after-tax return!

Crunching the Numbers
Calculating After-Tax Return on Two Index Funds

XYZ Synthetic Fund: $1,000 invested on January 1, 1998, earned 10% ($100) during 1998. The fund was sold on January 1, 1999. The investment return was taxed as regular income, thus the $100 earnings were taxed at Lana's *marginal tax rate* of 50% for regular income.

QRS Natural Fund: $1,000 invested for the same time period, earning the same rate of return, and sold on the same date. The investment return consisted of 3% dividends and 7% capital gain on the sale. The returns were taxed at Lana's marginal tax rate of 34% for dividends and 38% for capital gains.

The synthetic fund produced an after-tax return of $50. The natural fund produced an after-tax return of $63.20. Lana was surprised at the difference in the tax impact between the two similar funds. Without the advisor's counsel, she wouldn't have known the difference.

STRATEGY #8

Invest in Mutual Fund Corporations

A great advantage of an *RRSP* or *RRIF* is the tax-deferred compounding of income that occurs over time. Some *mutual funds* structured as corporations also give you some tax-deferred compounding — much like your RRSP or RRIF does — but in this case the *deferral of tax* is available outside an RRSP or RRIF.

Some mutual *fund companies* offer mutual funds structured through a *mutual fund corporation* rather than a traditional mutual fund trust. The corporation issues several classes of *shares*, with each share class investing in a different underlying mutual fund. You as an investor are permitted to switch among the share classes — this is similar to switching among different funds — without triggering a *capital gain*. As long as your investment remains within the corporate structure, any capital gains are deferred. If you redeem fund shares, however, this will trigger taxation on all gains and losses that have occurred.

One of the key advantages of these mutual fund corporations is the tax deferral on capital gains that is available to an investor who wants to actively manage his or her investment *portfolio* by switching among the different share classes. Note, however, that although the switching between classes is tax free, there may be tax consequences for the investor anyway. If the fund corporation has to sell stocks attributable to an existing share class in order to provide funds for the switch, taxable gains may find their way to the investors. This will ultimately depend on several factors, including the level of redemptions, capital gains and losses attributable to other share classes, and fund expenses.

▼

Example

Anna owns several *equity mutual funds* outside her RRSP. She likes to jump around between funds as she tries to time purchases and sales to take advantage of optimal performance, but for tax purposes she has been incurring capital gains each time she sells a fund (she is a successful investor!). She doesn't enjoy the tax she has been paying on these capital gains, so last year she looked into mutual fund corporations as an alternative.

Anna used cash from some matured *GICs* to purchase a balanced portfolio of mutual funds through a fund corporation structure. This year, when Anna prepared her tax return, she was pleased by the reduction in tax liability. The reduction was due to the elimination of some *interest* income from the GICs, and the fact that her mutual funds owned through the corporate structure were sheltering capital gains from tax she attracted each time she switched between funds.

Sure, tax will have to be paid on the eventual redemption of the investments, but in the meantime, a tax deferral is welcomed by Anna.

Crunching the Numbers

Anna's old equity funds: Anna sold equity fund A to buy equity fund B. A small gain was realized on the sale. Soon after, equity fund B was sold to buy equity fund C. A large gain was realized on equity fund B. This all happened in one month as Anna continued to make money in the market. It appears she is succeeding, as she made $2,000 of capital gains and $300 of dividends from her trading and her holdings.

Anna's new equity funds: In the same month, Anna flipped between three equity funds within the mutual fund corporation. She had similar success, again making $2,000 of capital gains and $300 of *dividends*.

While there appears to be no difference in profitability, when it is time to pay tax on Anna's successful investing, the $2,000 of capital gains earned inside the mutual fund corporation will not be taxed yet. These gains will be tax deferred until Anna eventually sells out of the new funds and the mutual fund corporation completely. The regular equity fund gains will cause $760 of tax to be paid next year, while none will be due on the new funds. A big difference!

STRATEGY #9

Think Tax Before Selling Your Non-RRSP/RRIF Mutual Funds

Remember when you filed your 1994 tax return and you *crystallized* accrued gains on your *non-RRSP/RRIF* mutual funds as of February 22, 1994? That crystallization produced an *exempt capital gains balance* for each fund, representing an account against which you can offset future *taxable capital gains* produced from that same *mutual fund*. That credit exists to help you to reduce future income tax incurred on capital gains either allocated from the fund or realized from the redemption of fund units.

You can utilize the account in two ways. One way is to use the account balance to offset any capital gains *distributions* made by the same mutual fund. An account balance can only be applied against distributions from that same fund elected on in 1994. The second way to use the account balance is when you actually sell fund *units* and realize a capital gain on the sale. The account balance can be used to offset the capital gain realized on the sale.

All of this means that you have the ability to earn tax-free capital gains generated by a mutual fund until the exempt gains balance is nil. If all the remaining units of a fund on which you claimed the capital gains exemption are sold and an exempt gains balance remains after the final sale, the remainder is added to the cost base immediately prior to the fund sale, producing a *capital loss* which can be used to offset other capital gains.

When you are determining which funds to sell, one of the things to look at is whether a related exempt gains balance exists. The existence of this account increases your after-tax return on the funds, so in some cases it may make sense to sell these funds before you sell others that have no exempt gains balance.

But remember, tax is only one of the factors to consider in deciding to sell investments. If you expect good performance in the future, a current sale (albeit tax free) means you may forfeit possible future returns, which could offset the immediate tax savings.

▼

Example

Tracy had decided to take a three-month vacation to the Far East, and was deciding how she would pay for the trip. She had a collection of *equity mutual funds* which she had saved over the last five years, and decided she would sell a portion of these funds to pay for the vacation. Tracy contacted her investment advisor and asked him to sell some of the funds to produce cash of $5,000. She didn't care which funds he sold, and thought he should know what was best. He said he would review her *portfolio* for funds that made sense to sell, and they agreed on a meeting date to conclude on what to sell.

That night, Tracy was having dinner with her parents and told them she was looking forward to her trip. Her father, a partner with a local chartered accounting firm who was also Tracy's accountant, asked how she was going to pay for the vacation and offered to help her with a loan until she returned. Tracy said thanks but explained that she was selling some of the mutual funds she had accumulated over time. Her father, knowing the tax treatment he had given Tracy's mutual funds in her tax returns over the years, suggested that he review her mutual funds from a tax point of view to determine which would be the best to sell. He said he would do this before her meeting with the investment advisor. Tracy admitted that she had not thought about the tax side of selling.

The next day, Tracy's father stated that several of the capital gains on her funds had been crystallized in 1994 and had large exempt capital gains balances. The sale of these funds would reduce her tax liability, leaving her with more money in pocket for her trip.

Armed with this information, Tracy visited her investment advisor to determine which funds to sell. In the end, they were able to sell some of the funds that had exempt capital gains balances (funds that were sensible to sell now in any case). In a few cases, the exempt gains balances reduced her capital gains significantly, and in one case, a capital loss arose (because the exempt gains balance had a remainder) which offset more of the capital gains.

Because of the tax reductions, Tracy didn't have to sell as many of her investments as originally anticipated to produce the $5,000 she needed for her vacation.

Crunching the Numbers

Tracy's portfolio that was sold:

Fund	Proceeds	Cost Base	Exempt Gains Balance	Remaining Capital Gain
AXL Equity Fund	$2,600	$1,000	$1,000	$600
BMC Equity Fund	$2,000	$1,000	$200	$800
XJF Equity Fund	$1,200	$1,100	$1,500	($1,400)

Selling this portfolio will generate proceeds of $5,800 and no taxation since the capital loss that results from the remainder of the exempt gains balance for XJF Fund offsets all other capital gains that are taxable.

STRATEGY #10

Should You Buy Bond Mutual Funds or Bonds?

Should you own *fixed income mutual funds* ("*bond funds*") or should you purchase *bonds* directly? Did you know that many of the bond investments owned by bond mutual funds (e.g., Government of Canada bonds) can be purchased by you directly?

Bonds themselves are fixed income investments where the bond issuer is borrowing money from investors for a period of time and paying *interest* to the bond holder for use of the money. Bonds are rated for risk level and some can be actively traded in the marketplace. Market-traded bonds (Canada Savings Bonds are not market traded) vary in price according to changes in market interest rates. Depending on the change in rates, you have the potential to earn *capital gains* or losses if you sell a bond for more than you purchased it. If the bond is purchased and matures at *face value*, you simply earn the interest promised on the bond.

Bond mutual funds are mutual funds that invest primarily in different types of bonds and other fixed income investments. Generally, a bond manager's role is to purchase new bonds as old ones mature, and to buy and sell bonds actively in the marketplace in an attempt to generate capital gains in addition to the bond interest income. Bond funds generally produce interest income, with some potential capital gains (or losses), depending on the bond *fund manager's* ability to buy and sell effectively.

Here are some pros and cons of owning bonds and bond funds:

- If a bond fund is owned outside an *RRSP* or *RRIF*, active bond trading by the fund manager can produce *tax-advantaged* capital gains besides the regular bond fund interest income. (You can also earn capital gains when you own bonds directly, if you sell them before they mature and conditions are favourable.)
- Because someone else (the bond fund manager) is managing the buying and selling of investments, purchasing a bond fund can mean less investment management and may be attractive to less sophisticated investors.
- Bond funds may have enough money to enable them to purchase a diverse collection of bonds and fixed income investments. As with equity funds, *diversification* can help to reduce risk in some cases. Outside a bond fund, an investor may not have enough money to purchase a diversified *portfolio* of bonds, since minimum investment amounts may be $5,000 or more for each bond.
- Because a bond fund can be actively managed by a bond manager, the potential exists for higher returns (interest plus capital gains). Individual investors owning bonds directly may be hard pressed to commit the time and expertise to replicate the bond fund manager's commitment to making investors more money.
- Bond funds may allow you to access specialty investments such as global bonds, higher-yielding bonds, and *emerging market bonds*. Access to these bonds by you directly

may be limited due to their steep minimum investment amounts.

- Bond funds, because of their size and financial clout, may be able to purchase large amounts of bonds at a lower cost than would be charged to an individual investor buying just one bond. This cost savings may be passed on to the investor through the bond fund's returns.

- Bond funds can be expensive for investors capable of managing their own portfolio of bonds. Bond fund *MERs* average more than 1.5% annually — plus any *loads* paid to purchase or sell the funds.

- Owners of bond funds may not be aware of the risk associated with the bond investments held by the funds. Bond fund managers may add higher-risk corporate bonds or royalty trusts to their portfolios without the investors knowing — possibly resulting in higher-risk bond portfolios than is desired. Owning bonds directly lets you more directly control the quality of the bonds you own by evaluating their creditworthiness and other characteristics of the issuers.

- Owning bonds directly allows investors to buy now and lock in a *yield* (the rate of return on the bond) until the bond matures. In other words, you know exactly what you'll have at the end of the period. With a bond fund, someone else manages the bond portfolio and you have no control over rate of return or when the manager buys and sells.

- Bond funds are easier and less expensive to purchase than bonds. Bond funds can be purchased for as little as a few hundred dollars, while market-traded bonds may cost several thousand dollars each.

So what is right for you, bonds or bond funds? It depends on what you are comfortable with, based on all the characteristics of both, how much money you have, your *risk tolerance,* and your need for *liquidity*, among other factors. Owning bonds directly gives you better direct control over your investment; you control the quality, the rate of return, and the maturity date.

Generally, investors with small amounts to invest and long time horizons may want to consider bond funds, since these give wide diversification of investments for limited amounts of money. A longer-term investor may more easily tolerate ups and downs of a bond fund managed by someone else striving to get higher returns. And generally, investors with more money and a shorter time period to invest may want to consider owning bonds directly if they want to lock in their rate of return and know how much money they will have on a certain date.

▼

Example

Jack is 65 and has just retired. He has started looking at his retirement portfolio recently and is trying to structure his retirement-income cash flow. Aside from his RRSP, Jack holds a large amount of *GICs* that are maturing soon. He doesn't plan on using his RRSP proceeds for several years and is happy with its current investment content.

Jack has heard about bonds and bond mutual funds and would like to utilize these investments to replace at least part of his GIC portfolio. He met with his investment advisor and they discussed the pros and cons of all of these fixed income investments, reviewed Jack's risk preferences, examined his overall *asset* mix, and determined his goals and cash needs. They developed an investment strategy that pleased Jack. Jack's strategy is outlined as follows:

- 20% of Jack's GIC portfolio will remain in GICs because he is used to GICs and isn't comfortable giving them up completely for something new. These GICs and the bonds described below will serve Jack's short-term (less than three years) cash needs.

- 50% of the GIC portfolio will be converted into five Government of Canada bonds of equal amounts, maturing each year for the next five years. The laddered strategy appeals to Jack because he wants to plan his cash flows for the next few years and having the fixed amounts mature one a year will provide an exact amount to be available to him each year.

- 30% of the GIC portfolio will be converted to a bond mutual fund holding high-quality bond investments. The bond fund is viewed by Jack as a five- to ten-year investment, where Jack is prepared to take a bit more risk by using an active bond manager in the hope of obtaining enhanced returns over that period of time. It's capital that Jack doesn't need to spend, and he can tolerate some ups and downs in that time period.

STRATEGY #11

Think Twice About Balanced Mutual Funds

A balanced *mutual fund* often uses a single *money manager* who tries to beat the market on a combined *stock* and *bond portfolio* held within a single fund. However, the reality is that most money managers have expertise in picking either the stock portfolio or the bond portfolio — but rarely both. So why not take maximum advantage of money manager expertise and invest with two "specialist" *fund managers*, each having a different specialty focus (stocks or bonds). Putting together a portfolio of specialist money managers decreases the likelihood of average returns resulting from using balanced managers who are good at several things but great at none.

If you are considering balanced mutual funds as part of your investment strategy, don't just look at the "positive" promotion — be aware of the not-so-widely known risks.

1. Higher Risk From Lack of Diversification
Let's take this idea of hiring specialists even further. You not only increase the likelihood of better returns, but also may

reduce the risk of loss from lack of *diversification*. Diversification is not limited to different classes of *assets*; you can diversify by applying different styles of investing (value versus growth, for example) or by investing in different regions of the world. Hunting out specialists to deal with different asset classes, different styles, and different geographic locales, allows you to put together an all-star team, managing a highly diversified portfolio that goes the extra mile to minimize risk and maximize returns.

An argument used for investing in *balanced funds* is that they provide the investor with built-in diversification. However, with a bit of effort, most investors can put together a specialist *bond fund* manager and a specialist *equity* fund manager in the same general proportions as the balanced fund to achieve similar diversification, but perhaps better returns.

2. Higher Fees

All this talk of hiring specialist managers for different asset groups may sound expensive, but you're in for a pleasant surprise. According to our research, the average mutual fund *management expense ratio* (MER) is 2.2% for Canadian equity funds, 1.7% for bond funds, and 2.3% for global equity funds. The average MER for balanced funds is 2.2% (Paltrak Mutual Fund Software 1998, Portfolio Analytics Ltd.). Based on these averages, using specialist money managers in a portfolio that would resemble a balanced fund (40% Canadian equity, 40% bond fund, and 20% global equity fund), you will have a weighted average MER of only 2.02%, and you can actually save money by investing in separate asset classes.

3. Lack of Concern for Tax and Investment Income

It makes good tax sense to hold highly taxed *interest*-bearing investments inside *tax-sheltered* plans (such as *RRSPs* and *RRIFs*) and equities that generate tax-advantaged *dividends*

41

and *capital gains* outside these plans. Unfortunately, this tax-saving strategy isn't possible when you own a balanced fund because the asset classes are combined in one investment. Owning separate equity and bond funds lets you plan more effectively by allowing you to defer tax on interest by holding the bond portion of your portfolio inside registered plans.

4. Inflexibility

Not only are balanced funds generally not tax efficient, they also don't offer the investor much flexibility. To withdraw cash from your balanced fund you must sell *units*, which means that the fund manager may sell both bonds and equities that are held in the fund. It makes more sense to invest in different asset classes separately, so that you can choose which class to sell when cash is needed. This puts more control in your hands and can result in less tax.

5. Failure to Add Value Through Management of the Asset Mix

Another argument you may hear supporting balanced funds is that having different asset classes within one fund allows the money manager to shift the asset mix depending on which asset classes are expected to perform better in the future. Well, an article by Marc Rouillard published in *Benefits Canada* (June 1993), sums up an interesting view on this argument. In referring to a study that assessed the timing of asset-mix shifts by Canadian balanced money managers between 1982 and 1991, he stated, "Canadian balanced fund managers, as a group, aren't improving returns through their timing bets. . . . On average, where the manager had full discretion, value was *subtracted* from balanced funds through active timing of asset mix shifts."

6. Disregard for Personal Investment Needs and Personal Characteristics

Investing in a balanced fund may be seen as the "easy way out" for some investors because the decision to invest between asset classes is delegated to the money manager. But that decision is not made with your particular personal financial needs in mind. Aren't you better off constructing your own personal portfolio of funds, where the allocation percentage between asset classes matches your financial goals? Choosing asset classes to invest in depends on your cash flow needs (bonds can generate more regular cash flow than some equities), your tax position (interest is taxed differently than dividends and capital gains), your investment time horizon (typically equities are more heavily weighted for a long-term investor than bonds or cash), your risk profile (there is greater volatility with equities than with fixed income or cash), your *liquidity* needs (use cash equivalents for short-term needs), your retirement needs, and other personal factors.

Your "perfect" portfolio is made up of a mix of investments specific to you, and should be used as your "blueprint" for investing, your measuring stick for your investment *performance*, and your re-balancing tool to adjust the asset allocation from time to time as your needs change.

By building your asset mix around your personal situation, the allocation percentages used in your portfolio take on a much greater significance.

▼

Example

By ages 50 and 52 respectively, Lynda and Brian had accumulated sizable *RRSPs*, and they thought it was time to get a second opinion on their investments, regardless of their

43

fairly good investment performance recently. After all, this was their life savings, and they were counting on this money to get them through retirement. If anything was worthy of a second opinion, it was this.

Sitting down with Arat, a financial advisor that a friend had recommended, Lynda and Brian showed her a *net worth* statement they had put together. Their RRSPs, totaling $400,000, consisted of two balanced mutual funds from two different money managers. Their non-RRSP savings comprised more of one of the balanced funds, and amounted to $75,000.

Lynda and Brian explained to Arat that their current advisor liked balanced funds, as they allowed them to "dip their toes" into stock market investing. Also, owning a simple balanced fund gave them an instant balanced portfolio. They had never invested in stocks before, and were nervous about doing so. Balanced funds owned some stocks, but also owned some bonds. They liked this.

Lynda said the non-RRSP money was there in case of immediate cash needs, but that the money seemed to be growing faster than it was being used. Still, they liked to have access to such a large amount.

Arat said that these balanced fund investments were not suitable for Lynda and Brian's needs. Lynda and Brian were surprised. They asked Arat to explain. Here is what Arat said:

• Your current advisor has ignored the specifics of your personal *risk tolerance*. When you buy a balanced fund, the money manager alone decides the mix between stocks and bonds. Sure, there may be guidelines for the fund, but the money manager may be able to own as much as 75% stocks in these balanced funds. Since you have two balanced funds, if we assume both funds can own up to 75% stocks, that means 75% of your $400,000, or $300,000, could be invested in stocks at any given time. Knowing this, are you comfortable with this level of potential exposure to the stock market?

- Your current advisor has ignored your liquidity needs outside your RRSP. You have told me that you like to have the investments outside your RRSP available for spending. A balanced fund should not be used for this purpose — the balanced fund owns stocks, and stocks should be purchased only where you know you won't need the money for five years or more. That way, when you need the money, the likelihood of selling the fund the day after a market drop is reduced. While the balanced fund owns bonds that are the right type of investment when planning for liquidity needs, the bonds in the balanced fund are attached to the stocks, and you can't sell one without the other. For your short-term liquidity needs, this money should be completely invested in a more liquid investment like bonds. Or the money in the balanced fund should be split in half, with some invested in stocks for the longer term, and the rest in bonds or money market investments to plan for the short-term cash needs.

- Your current advisor has ignored *tax-planning* opportunities in creating this portfolio. Balanced funds generate tax-friendly capital gains and dividend income from the stock portfolio, and tax-unfriendly interest income from the bond portfolio. Since the balanced fund owns both stocks and bonds, you are not able to separate the stocks from the bonds, and put the tax-unfriendly bonds inside your RRSP where the interest is tax sheltered. You could leave some of the stocks outside your RRSP where the capital gains and dividends would attract less tax. Keep in mind this objective must be balanced with the liquidity need we discussed.

Arat was going to explain about the higher annual cost of the balanced funds, when Lynda interjected and asked what they should do.

Arat explained how she could assist them to re-organize their portfolio to better match their risk tolerances and liquidity needs, as well as reduce the tax they pay on *investment income*. Lynda and Brian decided they would talk to their existing advisor about these ideas, and get back to Arat for any additional assistance they may need, or if they have any further questions.

STRATEGY #12

Investigate Oil and Gas Royalty Trusts

Oil and gas royalty *income trusts* have become a popular investment recently. Here is a summary of observations about their characteristics and their pros and cons, to help you understand them better.

- Oil and gas royalty income trusts are investment funds that permit *unit holders* (investors) to share in the production from oil and natural gas reserves. The future net cash flows earned from oil and gas production and sales are paid to such a *trust* as royalties. The trust may distribute most of the royalties it receives as cash *distributions* to unit holders.

- The revenue received in the trust can be reduced by special tax deductions available to resource operations, and the result is that part or all of the cash flow distributed by the trust in the initial years is treated as a capital distribution (a return of the original investment) of the trust, which is not subject to tax when received by the investor. Rather, the capital receipts reduce the cost base of the investor's trust *units* and may result in a larger *capital gain* on the eventual sale of the units. Many investors incorrectly assume that the distributions are all income and simply attract a lower level of taxation. The amount of tax payable on this investment can increase as the level of income distributed to the unit holder increases, and also when the units are eventually sold by the unit holder. This means that these trusts offer a *deferral of tax* when owned outside an *RRSP* or *RRIF,* and a potential capital gain on the sale of the units in the future.

• The trust is producing oil and gas from a depleting resource; in essence, an investor's capital is being returned with the production. If the trust does not replenish the oil and gas reserves with new properties, improve production methods, or benefit from increased prices, the investor may be left with nothing in the future. After all, the trust unit holder has no guarantee that the oil wells will continue to produce.

• Consumers should be cautious when comparing these returns to traditional *bond* or other fixed income investment returns. Oil and gas trusts can be affected by risks such as oil and gas price changes, market fluctuations, and declining production. These factors and others can affect distributions and the value of the trust units. This means that an oil and gas trust unit can behave more like an *equity* investment than a fixed income bond; you may need to evaluate it in that light in completing an assessment of risk and return for your investments. Another factor to consider when comparing returns is that the quoted annual returns of these trusts may include the return of your own capital, which is not an earned return, while other investments will quote only earned returns.

• Other factors that can be important to a trust's market value are the reserve life of the oil and gas properties, the quality of the reserves, the rate of decline of the reserves, and what portion of the investment return is a return of capital. Changes in these and other variables may lead to increases or decreases in the market value of units, resulting in a potential capital gain or loss if the investment is sold.

Oil and gas trusts can serve investors seeking an income tax deferral for a period of time. They can also serve investors in need of large cash distributions, but the investors must realize that the life of the oil and gas reserves is not guaranteed and therefore neither are the cash distributions.

Oil and gas trusts, along with several other variations of income trusts, are very popular today. They are complex investment vehicles that can carry some risk. Ensure that you talk to a qualified professional advisor with access to research on the products you are considering, who has access to a wide range of products for comparison, and has a strong understanding of the tax, cash-flow, and investment ramifications of these products. Because an oil and gas trust defers tax, it is important that you understand the tax impact over the years you own the product — including the tax impact when you eventually sell.

Do your homework on these relatively new investments; don't get blinded by the flashy returns and apparently low tax bite!

Important to Note

A wide variety of income trust investments have been introduced recently. Whether these trusts hold interests in resource properties or other businesses, their basic tax and *investment income* treatment is similar to that of the oil and gas trusts discussed in this strategy.

Before investing in these new and complex investments, research with your advisor and accountant to understand all the pros and cons of what you are buying.

▼

Example

Josh has a large, well-balanced investment *portfolio* outside his RRSP, consisting of bonds, a variety of mutual funds, some *stocks*, and some *GICs*. He has accumulated these savings from an inheritance of $200,000 a few years back.

Recently Josh has been upset about the low *interest* rates available for his maturing GICs. He has heard of oil and gas royalty trusts and their potential for higher returns. Their potentially lower tax bill is also attractive. Josh's investment advisor, Mike, commented on royalty trusts as an alternative to some stock investments. Josh compared several oil and gas trusts, examining the quality of the management, life of reserves, and other aspects suggested by his investment advisor.

Portfolio *diversification* and tax minimization are important to Josh, but they are not the most important aspects of his investments. With a far-off retirement horizon, Josh has little need for the higher current distributions offered by the trusts. He decided to purchase a small amount of royalty trust units, limiting his purchase to approximately 5% of his overall portfolio — enough to get some tax deferral and additional investment diversification, but not so much as to increase portfolio risk beyond a level he is comfortable with. Because of the limited size of his purchase, Josh was comfortable with the risk exposure and was happy he still had the ability to achieve some tax deferral.

STRATEGY #13

Research Investing in Labour Funds

Labour-sponsored venture capital corporations (*labour funds*) offer yet another *asset* class for a diversified *portfolio*: venture capital. Labour funds, which operate much like *mutual funds*, have been approved by the federal and provincial governments for the purposes of making investments into private businesses in Canada.

To attract investors, labour funds can offer significant *tax credits*: up to 15% of the amount invested (to a maximum investment of $5,000) is rebated by the federal government and often another 15% by some provincial governments (these credit amounts can vary). Since these same labour funds may also be eligible for your *RRSP*, they offer an additional 50% *tax deduction* to investors in the top tax bracket in Canada, reducing the cost of a $5,000 investment to $1,000. The trade-off is that investors are often required to hold these investments for a minimum time period or else lose the federal and provincial tax credits, and the investments owned in the funds can be somewhat riskier.

When evaluating labour funds for purchase, consider the

following: if you stripped away the attractive tax benefits, would the investment stand on its own merits? Like mutual funds, there are newer labour funds and there are older labour funds, and you should examine past *performance* carefully — but not solely. Remember, past performance may not be an indication of future performance, so it is also important to understand future potential of the fund. Note that *investment risk* associated with labour funds can be high; some funds invest in emerging, young, private companies in search of money, companies that may not be able to obtain the funding any other way. When evaluating labour funds for purchase, review the risk level with your financial advisor and ensure that the amount of risk assumed is consistent with your preferences.

As when evaluating all managed investment products, you should be concerned with the quality of management. Management should be experienced and qualified to manage such a fund. Read the labour fund's *prospectus* to gather some background information on the fund management team. Other information can be obtained by talking to your investment advisor. Don't be afraid to ask questions!

And then there are fees and costs of the labour fund. Like in a mutual fund, the fund management charges the fund a fee to operate and manage it. This fee can be steep in some cases, due sometimes to the additional legwork required for management to find and investigate new private business opportunities. There may also be a diminishing redemption fee associated with selling a fund after a short ownership period. And there could be a loss of tax credits if the funds are sold early. Investigate all of the fees associated with the particular labour fund(s) you are interested in buying.

Labour funds can produce a sizable tax deduction for your RRSP and some desirable tax credits as well, but purchase amounts should be well thought out. Don't lose sight of the importance of the investment just because of a tax write-off. Investigate the quality of the investment before buying. This type of investment can be a welcome part of a balanced investment portfolio, but do your homework before buying, and consider seeking the advice of a qualified investment and tax advisor to assist you with the decision.

▼

Example

Marian was shopping for her RRSP investments in February two years ago, and the significant tax breaks associated with labour-sponsored venture capital funds were hard to ignore. She was sold on the large tax credits offered in addition to the RRSP deduction. Marian really dislikes giving Revenue Canada any money, so these investments seemed like a good option. Marian bought $3,500 worth of one fund that year and another $3,000 the next year. This year, Marian is pondering the purchase of another labour fund investment, to add to her existing holdings in her $12,000 RRSP.

Looking back on last year, Marian now sees that she got caught up in the tax savings and ignored the investments behind the tax write-off of her labour funds. That year, the *TSE 300* returned 15%, while her two labour funds returned significantly less. Much of her tax savings from the initial investment were offset in one year of poor performance. Furthermore, she can't even switch funds now because of the redemption fees and loss of credits if she sells the labour funds early. So now she is concerned that these higher-risk investments will continue to underperform versus the markets and cost her more and more in lost returns that will eventually surpass her initial tax benefits. She is concerned that she may never have enough for retirement at this rate.

Marian's new financial advisor pointed out to her that a labour fund should be viewed as a long-term investment and

53

that returns may be volatile based on the risk level of the fund. He suggested that Marian wait another three to five years to assess the performance of the funds fairly. Her existing labour funds had been selected without any research at all, and without any consideration for *risk tolerance* and the rest of her investment portfolio. He suggested that this year, Marian should consider balancing her total RRSP portfolio by adding some bonds and blue-chip *equity mutual funds* according to a risk assessment and asset mix they could design together. He stated, however, that labour funds can form a suitable piece of a well-balanced investment portfolio. They could even consider purchasing some additional labour funds this year, after a thorough evaluation of Marian's needs and alternatives.

STRATEGY #14

Diversify into Real Estate Investment Trusts

Real estate investment trusts or REITs are publicly traded *closed-end trusts* or *trusts* that own, operate, acquire, and develop or finance real estate properties. "Closed-end" means that unlike in a mutual fund trust, there is a limit on the availability of the trust units. Most REITs invest in private and commercial real estate ranging from residential properties and regional malls to office, industrial, and health care properties. Here is a list of some of their characteristics, to assist you if you are considering a REIT purchase:

- Liquidity — Unlike pure real estate investments, publicly traded REITs trade on *stock exchanges*, making them much easier to sell than a single rental property.
- Diversification — Owning a REIT or several REITs means that you may own a share of properties across a region, a country, or a continent, helping to cushion the effect of suddenly depressed market conditions that may occur in any one area. This *diversification* may be preferable to owning one property in only one city.

- Effective management — Many U.S. REITs are fully functioning businesses, with management owning a percentage of the outstanding *shares*. Many Canadian REITs still hire management on a fee basis. Ownership by management can mean a greater devotion by management to be successful.

- Inflation fighter and a growth investment — REITs are a separate *asset* class and add effective diversification to a *stock* and *bond* portfolio. Rising rents and growing property values make REITs a growth investment and an *inflation* fighter.

- Defensive investing strengths — REITs are a good defensive choice in a rising or high stock market; because of high cash *yields*, they hold their value better in down markets. REITS are, however, subject to changes in *interest* rates, market growth, and real estate markets, and are not guaranteed investments.

- Some tax deferral — A portion of Canadian REIT distributions can be tax deferred as a result of capital cost allowance claimed by the REIT. Capital cost allowance is a notional non-cash expense to represent usage of a property (known as *depreciation* for accounting purposes). The capital cost allowance reduces taxable income but doesn't affect cash *distributions* to the *unit holder*. Unfortunately, this same capital cost allowance may be applied to reduce the cost base of the investment, potentially resulting in a *capital gain* on the eventual sale of the investment. But at least it may be a *tax-advantaged* capital gain! In addition, the capital cost allowance claim may result in *recapture*, which is taxed as *regular income* when the individual real estate property is sold.

- Ownership of a non-depleting asset — With oil and gas royalty trusts, the properties indirectly owned by the trusts are depleted. With REITs, on the other hand, you have a permanent investment that can continue to pay rental income and also have potential for capital growth on the value of the investment.

- A low-hassle investment — Professional management teams run REITs and the investments they hold. Compare this to rental properties, where you might be out cutting the grass every other week!

- Trust structure, not corporate structure — This leaves investors at risk of unlimited liability in the case of any large lawsuits against REIT properties. Check that the REIT management has property, casualty, and liability insurance as well as effective investing policies and other safeguards in place to minimize investor exposure to loss.

Like other stock market investments, REITs will fluctuate in value over time. The value of a REIT should be evaluated on all its merits and faults by you and a financial advisor experienced in REITs. Consider consulting a tax professional in order to completely understand the tax impact of REITs during the period you will own one (if held outside an *RRSP* or *RRIF*), and the tax impact on *disposal* of such an investment.

▼

Example

John was interested in adding some real estate to his non-RRSP investment portfolio and was considering purchasing a rental apartment building. John already had a large portfolio and felt the addition of real estate in some form would be diversification into an asset class he didn't currently hold. This added diversification, plus the inflation-fighting ability offered by the potential for rising rental income (through higher rents), was attractive. John admitted to his investment advisor, however, that he wanted a "low-maintenance" investment. The advisor said that owning his own rental property would require maintenance and upkeep, unless he was prepared to use a management company, which could prove costly. When the investment advisor noted that the disadvantages of personal real estate ownership include potentially poor *liquidity* if the property is hard to sell, and the uncertainty of performance of regional real estate markets, John decided to reconsider his purchase of his own real estate investment. Owning a rental property was attractive, but didn't seem to fit his lifestyle.

John wasn't aware of REITs until his investment advisor told him about them. John was attracted to the pros and could live with the cons of a Canadian REIT, and made a purchase for his portfolio after researching REITs with his advisor. The REIT seemed to offer all the advantages of a single rental property with few of the disadvantages. John's investment advisor had told him that owning a REIT would diversify his investment portfolio, would act as an inflation fighter, and might prove to be a growth investment. The REIT would be a growth investment if the rental properties owned by the REIT appreciated in value over time and this value was reflected in an increased value of John's REIT investment.

When John was shopping for a REIT investment, his advisor discussed the advantages of owning REITs investing in a variety of properties, in a variety of regions in a country, and even in several countries. If this diversification was not available from one REIT, the advisor suggested purchasing more than one REIT. The REIT that John and the advisor chose invested across Canada, providing exposure to several diverse real estate markets. John and the investment advisor also inquired about management quality, and compared the fee levels of several REITs before John purchased.

Finally, they investigated the extent to which *leveraging* or borrowed money was used to purchase investments in the REIT. They were concerned that the REIT might borrow excessively in order to purchase more properties. John and his advisor examined the REIT's financial statements and were satisfied that the REIT's leverage was not excessive. This opinion of the leverage was reaffirmed by discussions with the REIT management and John's accountant.

As with any investment, shop around for the best prices, and understand the differences among REITs in the marketplace. A REIT investment is an option for a well-balanced investment portfolio seeking diversification into an additional asset class.

STRATEGY #15

Take Advantage of Dividend Reinvestment Plans and Direct Share Ownership

Individuals who purchase an *equity mutual fund* purchase a collection of investments consisting primarily of *stocks* of public companies. So have you ever thought about owning those same stocks directly? Why not bypass most of the fees? Why not take advantage of free subsequent purchases?

Investing in stocks directly has several advantages. First, it eliminates the fees that your mutual *fund manager* charges you each year for managing your mutual fund *portfolio* (both the *load* fee and the internal fund *MER*). This alone may increase your rate of return 2% every year that you own shares directly. Second, you can purchase the stock investment fresh; in other words, your purchase price is your cost, and any future appreciation is earned by you and you pay tax on it. With mutual funds, you buy fund *units* that hold existing investments — investments which may have *accrued capital gains* you didn't earn but may pay tax on when sold (see Strategy #4). Third, you control the timing of the taxes associated with any capital gains you earn. With a mutual fund, your fund manager buys and sells stock when he or she wants to, and you face the tax liability when this happens. But if you purchase the stock directly and practise a *buy-and-hold* strategy, you can defer any capital gains until you decide to sell.

Yet another benefit of buying a company's stock directly is that you may be able to get involved in *dividend reinvestment plans* offered by the company. This is where any *dividends* you earn can be automatically reinvested to purchase more shares. While you still have to pay tax on these dividends, remember that dividend income is *tax-advantaged* income: outside your *RRSP* or *RRIF* you will pay less tax on dividend income compared to other types of income. Reinvesting dividends can be a powerful investment strategy because the reinvestment compounds the growth of your investment at an increasing rate as each year more dividends are earned and reinvested. Note that reinvestment of dividends is also available with mutual funds.

Thus, the strategy of buying *shares* directly has its merits, but here is a word of caution: buying mutual funds is usually more appropriate for investors who don't have enough money to purchase a diversified portfolio of stocks directly. Buying only a few stocks is far more risky than purchasing a mutual fund which may hold a diversified portfolio of 40 or more stocks. So what should you do? Well, if you really want to own some *equities*, consider buying shares in the big blue-chip companies in Canada that constitute lower-risk investments and offer dividend reinvestment plans. Speak to your investment advisor about a sample of these types of stocks.

And one other word of caution: while buying stocks directly can be a less expensive method of investing, in many cases it comes without professional investment advice. Depending on your investing sophistication, an investment advisor may add value by assisting you in evaluating what to buy, and when to eventually sell.

▼

#15 / Take Advantage of Dividend Reinvestment Plans and Direct Share Ownership

Example

Outside his RRSP, Trevor had a diversified portfolio of bonds and mutual funds totalling $500,000. He wanted to use part of this money and invest in some specific stocks that he believed would be solid long-term investments. Using his investment advisor, he purchased 1,000 shares in ABC Bank (paying a 2% commission to do so) and had the shares registered in his name so that he personally could enrol in the company's dividend reinvestment plan and optional *share purchase program*.

Normally, shares purchased through investment advisors and their firms are held in *street name* (not your name), and dividend reinvestment and additional share purchases made directly from the company may not be available. Why would your investment advisor want to give you access to free purchase? Some brokerages do offer free dividend reinvestment, however.

Trevor was also attracted to the optional share purchase program offered by his new investment in the bank. His advisor pointed out that many public companies in Canada (and many more in the U.S.) permit investors to make additional cash contributions to the company directly to purchase more shares with no fees. This is a great feature; some companies even let investors buy additional shares at a discount to market value.

The low fee cost of his new investment is appealing to Trevor, but the new record-keeping responsibilities are not. Since he owns the stock directly, he is also responsible for the administrative burden of keeping track of purchases, sales, reinvestments, and the tax cost base of the investment. Owning this same investment through a *brokerage* account might have reduced this burden, since it likely has a computerized record-keeping system in place. But because Trevor has only one stock investment owned directly, he doesn't think the paperwork should be overwhelming. In the future, though, he will evaluate this administrative burden against the fee savings when considering his preferred purchase route.

STRATEGY #16

Use Prescribed Annuities for Tax Deferral

An *annuity* is a stream of payments received by an individual for a period of time. Individuals can purchase annuities with a lump sum of money that will be used to provide the stream of payments in the future.

An annuity can be a particularly effective investment for several reasons. First, owning an annuity requires little if any maintenance. The amount of the future payments is set when the annuity is purchased and no further investment management is required by the investor. For seniors, for example, getting a cheque every month may be the only involvement they desire in managing their investments. Using annuities to provide low-hassle retirement income can reduce the stress of investing for many people, by simplifying their financial picture.

Second, a *prescribed annuity* can provide a deferral of tax, particularly in the annuity's first few years. Each annuity payment received is a blend of *interest* income and a return of the invested money. With a regular annuity, a greater amount of taxable interest is received early in the term of the annuity. With a prescribed annuity, the taxable interest is spread equally over the life of the annuity, thereby deferring the payment of tax compared to the case of a regular annuity. For a senior who may be on a fixed income who is concerned about taxes, a prescribed annuity can provide an improved cash flow in the early years of receiving annuity payments.

Third, an annuity can be useful as an investment for beneficiaries who may lack control over their spending habits. For an individual who is concerned that his or her children may spend every penny of the *estate*, an annuity can be a low-cost way to deal with that concern. An individual can direct his or her estate to purchase a life annuity (an annuity that provides payments for the entire life of the beneficiaries). With a life annuity, the beneficiaries will receive a regular income stream but can never access the principal amount. This strategy can also be useful for providing for medically challenged dependents who may not be capable of managing their personal affairs.

It is important to note that the cost of an annuity may fluctuate with changes in interest rates. Consider looking into annuities when market interest rates are higher, as this may result in less expensive annuity costs and higher payments to the beneficiaries. Also, annuities come in several shapes and sizes — e.g., you can purchase an annuity that raises payments to adjust for *inflation* — and can be purchased from a variety of institutions. Investigate annuities carefully and thoroughly before deciding whether to buy, including doing an analysis of the size and stability of the company offering the annuity. (Remember, the payments may have to last 50 years!)

If you decide to purchase a large annuity for your needs, consider buying two annuities from two institutions to address your concerns about the risks of having all your money with one institution.

▼

Example

Ben and Rose have been talking to their financial advisor about simplifying their personal finances. At ages 77 and 79 respectively, they no longer have the desire to stay as involved in the regular decision making relating to their investments. This change of heart has been partly due to Ben's stroke six months ago. Ben had been the financial decision maker for the family, and since his stroke Rose has been concerned about his reduced desire and ability to focus on their family cash flows. They thought about asking their children for help, but the children live far away and Ben and Rose don't want to burden them. They would simply like to reduce their involvement in investment decision making.

Dana, their advisor, suggested that Ben and Rose consider purchasing a prescribed annuity with their taxable investments, while continuing to manage their tax-sheltered funds as *RRIFs*. She explained what an annuity is and what the advantages will be to Ben and Rose:

- The annuity will provide a level stream of payments on a regular basis that can help to provide Ben and Rose with the regular cash flow they need to live.
- The annuity is managed by an insurance company. Once Ben and Rose provide a lump-sum amount to purchase the annuity, they will have no ongoing management responsibility. The insurance company will provide them with regular payments according to the terms of the annuity. This arrangement meets Ben and Rose's desire to have less investment responsibility.
- The after-tax cash flow to Ben and Rose may increase in the short term since the annuity payments will consist of some income and a return of original capital. The capital

portion is not taxed. This additional cash flow will come in handy to pay for the expensive medical attention Ben is receiving as a result of his stroke.

Dana noted that many people worry about the continued solvency of Canadian insurance companies that sell annuities. While this is always a concern, she explained that they could purchase the annuity from one of Canada's largest institutions, or they could purchase two annuities from two different institutions, to further diversify and reduce risk of loss.

Finally, Dana suggested that Ben and Rose invest only a portion of the funds in an annuity. Like other types of investment, an annuity is an option where you may want to invest some money, but not necessarily all your money. A small investment will provide Ben and Rose with the many advantages of an annuity but will not leave them locked in with only one type of investment. Dana observed that Ben and Rose will continue to own RRIFs with their tax-sheltered investments, and Dana can continue to assist them in managing this part of their finances.

Rose liked this balanced approach. It would be less work for them. She wants to start looking at different annuity options immediately.

STRATEGY #17

Replace Mutual Funds with Pooled Funds

Pooled funds are similar to *mutual funds* but have higher minimum investment amounts. Pooled funds are consequently far less known in Canada than mutual funds, because the former are not available to the average Canadian. The minimum investment of at least $150,000 per fund is significantly higher than for mutual funds, which may have a minimum investment of $1,000. However, if you are someone with a growing investment *portfolio* or will likely inherit some wealth later in life, pooled funds may make sense for you as a replacement or supplement to your mutual fund portfolio.

Consider this: the average annual *management expense ratio* (MER) of an equity mutual fund in Canada is currently over 2%. And add to this any purchase or sale *loads* you might also pay associated with the mutual fund.

Now consider this: several pooled equity funds in Canada have MERs of approximately 1% or less, with no load fees. This means that you could own a similar investment, with a 1% saving every year! On a $100,000 investment in a pooled fund, you will save $1,000 every single year! This

$1,000 savings, when compounded at 8% for 30 years, will grow to $113,000!

Aside from their cost savings, many of the pooled funds currently available in Canada are available on a no-load basis. That is, there may be no fees to buy or sell such a fund. Despite fee and expense differences, pooled funds can hold the same investments as mutual funds and operate in a similar fashion. Some of the mutual fund companies you currently invest in may also offer pooled funds, and you may not know it!

A word on *diversification* and pooled funds: proper *asset allocation* strategies involve investing across several *asset* classes: Canadian equities, international equities, *bonds*, etc. Since pooled funds have a minimum investment per fund of at least $150,000, an investor likely needs at least $500,000 to develop a properly balanced portfolio of pooled funds. However, a pooled fund can be combined with mutual funds to achieve diversification more easily but potentially at a greater cost.

Investors who meet the minimum investment levels should consider pooled fund investments. Chances are, the mutual fund companies they currently invest with also have pooled funds consisting of similar investments.

▼

Example

Jody is just getting over the passing away of her father several months ago. Since he was predeceased by her mother, Jody now finds herself the sole beneficiary of their estate. In two weeks the family lawyer is sending her a cheque for $700,000 to cover the cash component of the estate. Jody approached her *financial planner* about options for investing the money.

Jody was going to buy mutual funds, until her financial

planner introduced her to pooled funds. She learned that she could purchase them without any upfront fees, switching fees, or deferred fees. Even better, she liked the fact that annual management expenses of the funds were generally 1% or 1.5% — compared to 2% or 2.5% for regular mutual funds. After she completed a risk assessment and developed a proper asset allocation mix, Jody and the financial planner reviewed several companies offering pooled funds, before settling on two. Jody decided to divide her money between two companies in order to reduce the risk of putting all of her money in one basket. Also, since each manager looked at investing in a different way, the division would further reduce risk. That way, one manager might have a good year while the other has a bad year, but with the combination Jody would be less likely to have a bad year overall. Investing with only one manager would increase the likelihood that Jody would have a bad investment year at some point in the future.

The financial planner smiled and together they proceeded to investigate the process of investing with these two pooled *fund managers*.

Crunching the Numbers

Given Jody's $700,000, saving 1% on fees means an extra $3,500 after-tax in her pocket every year. Over 20 years, compounded annually at 8%, this will accumulate to $170,000 pre-tax. In other words, fees matter!

STRATEGY #18

Understand the Difference Between Funds, Pools, and Segregated Money Management to Save Taxes

Investors in Canada have three broad choices of investments. We have explored the characteristics of different types of *mutual funds*, and we have discussed some potentially disadvantageous tax issues (see Strategies #2 and #4) associated with mutual funds.

We have also discussed *pooled funds* (see Strategy #17) and how they differ from mutual funds. Unfortunately, pooled funds have the same tax issues as mutual funds, so that the weaknesses of mutual funds discussed in Strategies 2 and 4 also apply to pooled funds.

Segregated Money Management

Segregated money management differs from mutual funds and pooled funds, because inside a segregated account you own specific investments, as opposed to fund *units*. Therefore, when you set up a *portfolio*, the investments inside your account are purchased fresh for you. This is unlike a mutual fund, which may have *accrued capital gains* you didn't earn, but may have to pay tax on.

If you still aren't clear, segregated money management means individual ownership of the *stocks* and *bonds* in your portfolio. This differs from fund ownership, where you buy fund units that represent ownership, in a portfolio of stocks and bonds. You know you have segregated money management when you see the names of the stocks and bonds you own on your monthly statements. If you own a mutual or pooled fund, all you see is the name of the fund.

Why Does Segregated Money Management Matter?

Buying investments in a segregated format is advantageous from a tax point of view, compared to funds or pools, assuming you have enough money to afford this form of ownership. Holding individual stocks and bonds gives investors far greater control over the present and future tax liability that will result from this investment. For example:

- When you make your initial purchase under the segregated format, you know exactly what you pay for the individual stocks and bonds that go into your portfolio. But with mutual funds, as I described in Strategies 2 and 4, you purchase units that may consist of accrued gains that you didn't earn, but may pay tax on. Under segregated money management, investments are purchased anew, therefore you have control over your *adjusted cost bases* for tax purposes.
- Holding individual stocks and bonds on a segregated basis allows you or your *money managers* to decide what to buy or sell for your benefit. In a fund, the *fund manager* has complete authority over what to buy and sell, and may choose to ignore tax consequences. Therefore, segregated money management gives you greater personal control and flexibility to offset stocks with *capital gains* against stocks with *capital losses* to benefit you personally.

71

Or you and your money manager may decide to trigger some accrued losses each December to offset the gains you made in the year. It is this ability to control your tax bill to some extent that makes segregated money management attractive.

Why Isn't Everyone Investing on a Segregated Basis?

Despite the potential tax drawbacks, mutual funds and pooled funds remain the best type of investments for investors who have less than $1 million to invest. (Most of us!) Segregated money management is generally appropriate for investors with greater than $1 million to invest. At this wealth level an investor can purchase enough stocks and bonds, in a variety of industries, sizes, countries, *asset* classes, etc., to equal the powerful risk management feature that mutual funds offer through *diversification*. In a segregated account with less than $1 million, you will have better control over your tax liabilities down the road, but you are taking on greater *investment risk* (of loss) by spreading your money among fewer investments. Also, at lower wealth levels, it may cost you more in transaction fees to buy on a segregated basis, compared to what you would pay through a mutual fund that can access lower brokerage costs than you can as an individual.

Important to Note

The segregated money management discussed in this strategy is completely different from mutual funds offered through *life insurance* companies, which happen to be called segregated funds. Don't confuse the two!

Wrapped Segregated Money Management Products: The Next Generation

Today in Canada, segregated *wrapped investment products*, created mainly by the big *brokerages*, are becoming popular investments. There are two kinds: wrapped pooled products and segregated wrapped products. A wrapped product is an investment program where a number of professional money managers have been contracted to manage a piece of an investment portfolio. There may be a Canadian *equity* manager, a Canadian bond manager, an *international equity* manager, and so on, and each manager may be from a different company. Additionally, the wrapped product may have several managers within each asset class, each managing a piece (say, Canadian equity, for example) using his or her own style of investing or focusing on a particular size of company. This differentiation in style is a form of additional diversification that can reduce your investment risk.

Investors purchasing a wrapped product will be assisted by an investment advisor to formulate a strategic *asset allocation mix* based on risk and return profiles. The advisor will also assist with deciding which managers (from a stable within the wrapped product) will manage their money.

A wrapped product may be sold with a single fee, which may be tax deductible, and this fee can incorporate the transaction fees, custody fees, and any other costs associated with this product.

Here are some advantages of a wrapped product:

- Instead of having one money manager managing a fund, you may have access to several professional managers in one product. More diversification among many managers can reduce your investment risk.
- You are charged one annual fee based on the value of your investment. Fees based on the market value of the portfolio encourage the money manager to grow your

wealth. This may be preferable to you owning stocks and bonds, where a *broker* gets paid for buying and selling on your behalf and may sell more frequently to generate more *commissions*.

- With a segregated wrapped product, you are purchasing segregated money management as opposed to buying a pool or fund. This means that when you buy in, the investments inside your account are purchased fresh; you don't purchase a fund that may have accrued capital gains you didn't earn but may pay tax on — unlike those that may exist inside a mutual or pooled fund. (This only matters outside an *RRSP* or *RRIF*.)

- Reporting is generally good in a wrapped product. Many of the wrapped products provide personal rates of return on your investment and a benchmark against which you can compare returns.

- Wrapped products are available to investors with less than $250,000, in some cases. Normally, investors need more than $1 million to create a similar investment portfolio on their own.

Some disadvantages of a wrapped product include:

- Relatively high fees. The annual fee may be approximately 2% to 3% a year. Thus, on a $1,000,000 investment you may pay a fee of up to $30,000 each year. You must decide if you are getting $30,000 worth of value every year. For that fee, you do get access to more than just an investment product. In most cases, a financial advisor will assist you to determine your appropriate asset allocation, discuss the appropriate money managers for you, and be available for your ongoing investment needs.

- Also with respect to fees, be aware that few professional money managers can beat the indices (like the *TSE 300* and the S&P 500) consistently by 2–3%. If they can't beat an *index*, why not just buy an *index mutual fund* investment (with typical fees of about 0.5%) and save all the fees?

- Many of the wrapped products available have hired good money managers, but perhaps not all the best managers available for a particular asset class. Some of the exceptional managers are not available through wrapped products.

- Because a wrapped product is custom-made by the institution offering it, the investment may be difficult to transfer to another institution if you become unhappy with the present one. If you want to take your business elsewhere, you may have to dispose of your wrapped product and take the cash to your new advisor. Any selling of the wrapped account holdings outside an RRSP or RRIF attracts tax, and this is not desirable. This forced selling isn't always necessary, and in many instances you can transfer your portfolio out "as is" without triggering any tax. You'll want to clarify the rules about leaving before you buy and ask if there are any exit fees as well.

- While segregated wrapped products are generally available to investors with small amounts to invest, a money manager may face difficulty in creating a properly diversified portfolio in a cost-effective way with less than $500,000. Better investment diversification may be available through mutual or pooled funds.

- Investors interested in having a close relationship with the money manager directly, instead of through a financial advisor representing the wrapped product, will not be able to do so. While some institutions selling wrapped products will invite you to hear the money managers speak at seminars, this doesn't replace a personal relationship with the money manager who is investing your money.

If you are going to buy a wrapped product, shop around. Every institution seems to have one, each with a similar group of money managers, and each with similar fees. Compare at least three wrapped products before buying, in order to get a good understanding of each institution's process to invest your money in the wrap, the institution's commitment to customer service, and all the options of the products available. Decide whether the higher cost of these products is worth the pros according to your personal needs.

▼

Example

Suzanne had just won $5 million in a lottery, and after recovering from the surprise of winning, she decided to invest most of her prize for the long term. She set out on her own to investigate professional money managers, mutual funds, pooled funds, and wrapped accounts for her investment needs.

After a series of interviews, Suzanne concluded she would hire several professional money managers available through a brokerage segregated wrap program. Here are her reasons:

- With $5 million, she wanted the tax advantages associated with segregated money management. Mutual funds and pooled funds were useful when she had only $1,000 to invest, but now that she is ready for more advanced investing (and the attractive tax benefits associated with segregated investing), she wants to create her own segregated portfolio of stocks and bonds.
- Suzanne wanted the benefits of a multi-manager approach, so she ruled out hiring just one professional money manager. After all, if you can hire two great minds to manage your money, isn't two better than one? Two

separate managers using their own distinct management style in creating a portfolio will also help to mitigate investment risk since each manager's portfolio will rarely act the same way in the market. Hiring two managers allows you to compare the quality and wisdom of each, and each acts like a second opinion to the other.

• Suzanne learned that a particular money manager may be good only at a particular type of investing. She decided she wanted specialist managers for each piece of her portfolio: Canadian bonds, Canadian stocks, U.S. stocks, and international stocks. This meant she would probably need at least four money managers — all managing her money on a segregated basis. With only $5 million, she would be able to hire only two or three managers if she approached them directly. Through the brokerage platform, the usually high minimum investment amounts can be as low as $100,000 per money manager, and Suzanne is able to design a multi-managed investment portfolio for $5 million.

With the type of investment decided, Suzanne set out to pick money managers to manage the different pieces of her portfolio. In the end, she selected one Canadian *fixed income* manager and she purchased a bond index fund, two Canadian stock managers (a value manager and a growth manager), two U.S. equity managers (a value manager and a growth manager), and an international index fund.

Suzanne managed to purchase this entire program for less than 1%, through some tough negotiations with her advisor and the brokerage, and from comparison shopping. She likes the fact that this fee will also be tax deductible.

STRATEGY #19

Weigh TIPS for Your Equity Needs

Have you considered some *TIPS* as an investment alternative to *equity* funds and equity *index* funds? TSE 35 Index Participation Units or "TIPS" are created by the Toronto Stock Exchange to permit investors to own a piece of the TSE 35 Index. The TSE 35 Index consists of some of the largest and most heavily traded publicly listed companies in Canada and is a subset of the *TSE 300*. Ownership of the TSE 35 offers *diversification* geographically and across industries; it offers *liquidity*, as the *units* are easy to sell; and the TSE 35 Index offers the flow through of *dividends* paid by the companies owned by the units. Most of the 35 companies included in the TIPS index have a *market capitalization* greater than $1 billion, meaning that the TSE 35 is a holding of *blue-chip* Canadian equities. Over the period from February 1992 to February 1997, the annual return with dividends reinvested in TIPS has been 14.6%.

Since the Toronto Stock Exchange promises to cover all excessive management costs that may reduce an investor's *yield*, a TIPS investment has the benefits of a blue-chip mutual fund without the annual management fees (which currently average over 2% per year for Canadian equity funds). And since TIPS are fully invested in the index, there are no *money managers* required behind the scenes to buy and sell stocks. This means no worries about managers possibly leaving the fund.

TIPS pay dividends quarterly. Incoming dividends are held in an interest-bearing account until they are paid out, with the interest earned on the account going to pay administrative costs of operating TIPS. The Toronto Stock Exchange covers all unpaid expenses. Regular mutual funds pay all fees out of your returns, and also take a profit component for the fund company, all of which can together approach 3% a year. TIPS have no ongoing fees.

The TIPS *portfolio* is adjusted to reflect the changes in the TSE 35 Index. Historically, there have not been many changes in the composition of the index, meaning that turnover in your TIPS portfolio should be low — attracting less tax from fewer *realized capital gains.*

An additional note: TIPS have a brother called "TIPS 100," which are a similar investment created by the Toronto Stock Exchange to invest in the top 100 companies in the TSE 300 Index. TIPS 100 operate in a similar fashion to TIPS, except that you can obtain broader diversification since TIPS 100 invest across 100 large companies in a variety of industries.

Similar investments exist in the United States' stock markets as well. All of these investments represent excellent low-cost methods of purchasing a play on the major indices or portions of the major indices in Canada and elsewhere.

▼

Example

George owns several Canadian equity mutual funds inside his *RRSP*. Every February, George picks another fund for the Canadian equity component of his RRSP investment. This year, George has discovered TIPS, and he plans to purchase them for his *discount brokerage* account. He likes the diversified blue-chip portfolio offered by TIPS. He also likes the fact that there is no worry about a manager leaving the fund company. But most of all, he likes the cost savings, which work out as follows:

Estimated brokerage fee to purchase 300 TIPS units	
(300 units x $30/unit x 1%)	$90
Annual management cost of the portfolio	$0
Total year-one fee to own TIPS	**$90**
Total future fees to own TIPS	**$0**
Purchase price (2% front load) of a similar	
equity mutual fund	
(300 units x $30/unit x 2%)	$180
Annual management cost of the portfolio	
(300 units x $30/unit x 2.25%)	$203
Total year-one fee to own the fund	**$383**
Total future fees to own the fund	**$203/year**

STRATEGY #20

Replace Some GICs with Stripped Bonds

Guaranteed Investment Certificates or GICs are investments that provide a fixed amount of *interest* over a fixed period of time. They are generally not cashable prior to maturity, and may be guaranteed to some extent by the *Canadian Deposit Insurance Corporation* (CDIC).

Government *stripped bonds* are obligations of the federal or provincial government that are created when the semi-annual interest payments (the coupons) of a *bond* are separated from the bond itself to create two investment products from one. The separated bond coupon payments and the residual bond sell at a discount to their maturity value, and on maturity they pay out their maturity value. Both the coupon payments and the residue have come to be known as "stripped bonds."

There are no income *distributions* during the life of the separated coupons or residue, but rather the purchase amount increases in value annually until the maturity value is reached. This increase in value over a period of time determines the *yield* to maturity or the rate of return on the stripped bonds.

Note that for tax purposes, income in the form of accruing yield from the coupons or the residue is taxed annually, even though no actual income distributions are received until maturity (when the maturity value of the investment is received). This can create problems for individuals relying on timely income distributions to pay the tax due on the annual return. This negative tax aspect can make purchasing stripped bonds outside an *RRSP* or *RRIF* unattractive.

There are several reasons why you should consider purchasing stripped bonds for your RRSP or RRIF:

• Safety. Stripped government bonds offer the same credit rating and level of safety provided by a regular federal government or provincial government bond. This means that stripped bonds offer a full guarantee of principal and interest to maturity and likely come with an independent credit rating as to the quality of the bonds. Guaranteed Investment Certificates, however, may be guaranteed only up to $60,000 under the Canadian Deposit Insurance Corporation.

• Higher interest rate. The interest earned on a stripped bond may be higher than that on a GIC of comparable term. This is due to the fact that stripped bonds, unlike GICs, are traded in an open market, and within this market there is a wider variety of issuers with different characteristics, all of which have varying credit ratings, which impact return. Also, GIC interest rates, which are set by the institutions offering them, may not change as quickly as the Canadian bond market, which reacts immediately to factors warranting a change in value.

• *Liquidity.* Stripped bonds trade in the secondary market in Canada, and can be bought and sold relatively easily on a daily basis. Stripped bonds are not locked in until maturity, and they have good liquidity if you need the money. GICs, on the other hand, are locked-in investments.

- Tax advantages. GICs earn interest income, which is the most *tax-disadvantaged* type of income available in Canada. Stripped bonds earn interest income too, but have the potential to produce *tax-advantaged* capital gains and *capital losses*. (This tax advantage is not relevant inside an RRSP, however.) A *capital gain* or loss depends on what happens to interest rates in the marketplace after the bond is purchased. If rates fall after the bond is purchased, the bond becomes more attractive. This raises the market value of the stripped bond and a capital gain is possible if the bond is sold prior to maturity. On the negative side, the absence of regular interest income associated with regular bonds means that the value of stripped bonds is more volatile in relation to interest-rate changes in the marketplace. A rise in interest rates may result in a capital loss if the stripped bond is sold prior to maturity.

- Flexibility. GICs are typically available in up to five-year terms. Stripped bonds are available with terms ranging from less than a year to greater than 25 years. Stripped bonds can be tailored to a variety of investment needs through a combination of different maturities and face values. A stripped bond *portfolio* can be set up to have a bond mature in year one, year two, and so on, such that an entire portfolio can be structured to provide annual retirement income each year as needed. Additionally, a laddered portfolio as described can also be renewed over a period of time so that a large amount of the portfolio is never faced with reinvestment during a period of low interest rates.

- No reinvestment risk. Since stripped bonds don't pay anything before maturity, there is no worrying about how to reinvest income generated from the investment. This is unlike the situation with regular bonds, where an investor can find widely different interest-rate conditions in the marketplace when it comes time to decide what to do with the interest income generated each year from the bonds.

▼

Example

At age 45, Gordon had built a sizable portfolio of GICs in his RRSP, but he was not pleased with the recent low rates of return he was earning on these investments. While this fixed income portfolio was only part of his total investment portfolio, he was ready to look for fixed income investment alternatives.

Gordon had just read some material from his financial institution on stripped bonds. He liked the flexibility of being able to buy and sell whenever he wanted; and he liked being able to buy a 20-year bond. This option seemed particularly attractive because when interest rates were high, he could lock them in for a long time — much longer than the five years permitted by GICs. And he really liked the higher returns available on some stripped bonds.

Gordon got a second opinion on stripped bonds from his investment advisor. He decided he would introduce stripped bonds to his GIC portfolio gradually as the GICs matured. He would reinvest in stripped bonds and select a longer maturity date if interest rates were high and a shorter-term bond if interest rates were low. As a conservative investor, Gordon also decided to buy only Government of Canada stripped bonds, to ensure that he owned high-quality investments.

Gordon thought that it would be wise to utilize his financial institution's expertise with stripped bonds to help him understand what to do. So he and the institution set up a game plan to work together on Gordon's portfolio as he added the stripped bonds. The institution suggested that Gordon consider setting up a laddered bond portfolio — that is, purchasing stripped bonds that mature at regular time intervals over a period of years. That way, Gordon would have a bond maturing potentially each year that could be spent or reinvested. Such a portfolio could also prevent him from having all his fixed income investments mature in one year when interest rates were low and reinvestment at these low rates would not be desirable.

STRATEGY #21

Strategize with Employee Stock Options

Stock options are financial instruments provided by employers that give employees the right to purchase company *shares* at a specified price (*exercise price*) within a specified time period. When the options are *exercised*, the employee pays the exercise price in exchange for the shares, which generally are worth more than the exercise price. From a tax perspective, the difference between the exercise price and the market price of the shares at the time of exercise is taxed as *employment income* in the year the employee exercises the option, unless the company is a *Canadian controlled private corporation* (CCPC), in which case the employee won't be taxed until he or she disposes of the shares. In either case, the employee may be entitled to a *stock* option deduction on his or her tax return equal to 25% of the amount included in income, if certain conditions are met.

Stock options are a popular form of compensation because the amount of money an employee may eventually receive is tied to the success of the company as measured by share price increases. Thus, a stock option can be a good incentive for employees to chip in to produce a successful company. Many *corporations*, therefore, like to see employees hold their stock options for the long term, and the companies apply staged vesting periods directing the minimum holding period before the options can be exchanged for shares. This corporate expectation may, however, conflict with some employees' desire for a balanced investment strategy.

Many senior executives may hold significant amounts of options and company shares, which may create excessively risky *portfolios* since these executives' portfolios may not be well diversified. If the company stock takes a nosedive, so potentially does a significant part of the executives' life savings.

Stock Options and Investment Strategy

The value of stock options and company stock should be included in the determination of a balanced investment portfolio. If the company is a small private company, the company's options and stock should likely be considered as a higher-risk *equity* component of the portfolio. If the company is a *blue-chip* public corporation, the options may be considered less risky. Discuss the appropriate risk level of your company with a financial advisor. Overall, the company's options and stock should not make up an overwhelming portion of a portfolio, but rather should comprise a portion of the portfolio that meets your *risk tolerance* and *asset mix* expectations. This may require you to exercise some of the options, sell the stock, and re-invest in a more balanced investment selection in order to achieve this balance.

Stock Options and Tax Strategy

Any stock you own that has a large *accrued capital gain* will be taxed when the stock is sold and the gain is realized. Stock options, which may also contain accrued value, will be taxed when the shares that resulted from the option exercise for a private company are sold, or will be taxed when the options for a public company are exercised *and* possibly also when the resulting shares are sold. Strictly from a tax point of view, it is in an employee's best interest to hold existing stock indefinitely and to exercise options at the last possible moment in order to defer taxation. While no tax reductions may be achieved, this strategy will create a *deferral of tax* — perhaps the next best thing. But keep in mind that owning substantial options and shares of any one company may be risky due to a lack of investment diversification.

Stock owned by an employee should be gifted to his or her spouse prior to any further stock option exercise, in order to avoid an *averaging of the cost base* of all the shares. An averaging of the cost base would result in an acceleration of tax payable, since the existing shares likely have an actual cost that is lower than the cost of the new shares. Moving the older shares, which hold a larger accrued gain, to a spouse may permit the employee to sell the newer shares and pay tax currently on a smaller *capital gain*. The transfer of the other shares to the spouse does not attract immediate taxation because transfers between spouses are deemed to take place at cost. Note, however, that any income and capital gains from the shares gifted to the spouse will still be taxed in the employee's hands.

Share owners of Canadian controlled private companies have an additional option unavailable to public company share owners. Shareholders of private Canadian companies can use a $500,000 capital gains exemption available to every Canadian taxpayer to offset capital gains incurred on the disposal of CCPC shares. Accessing the exemption is not guaranteed, and the criteria should be reviewed with a qualified tax professional. Nevertheless, shareholders of qualifying corporations should make every attempt to take advantage of this exemption.

Overall, What to Do

Selecting a strategy to provide you with financial peace of mind requires you to balance your preference for tax deferral with your investment risk tolerance, while considering your cash-flow needs and any corporate expectations for you to hold options or own company stock. Does this sound like a juggling act? The following points are worth considering.

The first priority is to develop a balanced investment portfolio. Taking steps to protect your retirement nest egg is arguably more important than paying some tax today. This may mean reducing your holdings of options and stock. This can be completed with a lump-sum exercise, stock sale, and reinvestment into other investments, or with a once-a-year exercise-and-sell strategy that produces a more gradual move toward a balanced portfolio. One attractive approach is a series of exercise-and-sell strategies where you can buy other investments over a period of time, hopefully avoiding buying at a market high. Buying over time is a common purchase strategy which reduces risk of any significant losses compared to buying all at once. This series of exercise-and-sell strategies is attractive because employees can continue to share in the success of their companies during the period of exercise. In any case, the options typically expire at specific future dates, so it is important to keep these dates in mind so that you don't forgo any benefits. Employees who are retiring and will no longer be responsible for the success of the company may prefer to sell all their holdings before they retire.

A series of exercise-and-sell strategies can be attractive from a company's point of view also, since the company may prefer this to an all-out dumping of its options and stock. A large sales volume might be perceived negatively by other shareholders and could hurt share price where such transactions are published in newspapers. Selling over a period of time can be more politically friendly and less likely to be noticed publicly.

The second consideration is taxation. Another drawback to exercising and selling all at once is the high level of taxation that would occur. A strategy of exercising and selling over time permits the employee to continue to defer some taxation to a later date. An employee should take steps to utilize the $500,000 capital gains exemption if the shares resulting from the exercised options are for a private qualifying company. As mentioned above, however, existing shareholdings should be gifted to a spouse (or transferred to a holding corporation) before any exercising, in order to minimize and defer tax.

Stocks options and company stock can be a significant portion of an employee's investment portfolio. It is in your best interest to consult a professional advisor who understands all the issues rather than just exercising and selling at will.

▼

Example

Roberta is a senior vice president with a large public company in Canada. Her *RRSP* totals $200,000 and consists mostly of company stock, currently valued at $150,000, which has greatly appreciated over the last five years. Roberta also has several thousand company stock options which can be exercised each year for the next five years, and she owns a small amount of stock outside her RRSP.

Roberta's corporation likes to have its executives own corporate shares but does not force the employees to own large amounts. Roberta was uncomfortable with having so much of her RRSP portfolio invested in only one stock investment. She was also unfamiliar with the tax rules for stock options, and wanted to develop a strategy to deal with any tax concerns. After consulting her *financial planner* and a tax accountant experienced with stock option strategies, Roberta decided on the following plan:

1. She would sell 75% of the company stock in her RRSP and invest the proceeds in a combination of government *stripped bonds, equity mutual funds,* and *Treasury bills,* based on an *asset allocation* assessment completed by her financial planner. She would sell in four instalments over two years, which would permit her to continue to share in the anticipated company stock price increase expected in the next year. Roberta was confident of this share price increase, based on her experiences in the company and corporate plans for the next year. There would be no tax issues for this stock sale since the investments are held inside Roberta's RRSP.

2. She would transfer the non-RRSP stock to her husband, Ali, in order to avoid the averaging of her cost base between these shares and her newly exercised shares discussed below. For tax purposes, these existing shares could be transferred to Ali at cost. This would serve to minimize taxes paid, by permitting her to realize the smaller capital gains on the sale of the newer stock holdings rather than the larger gains from the averaging of cost with the older stock holdings now in her husband's name.

3. Roberta's tax accountant pointed out that Roberta would have to pay tax on any dividend income and future capital gains earned on the shares gifted to Ali.

4. Finally, Roberta would set up a plan to exercise 20% of her options and sell the shares each year for the next five years. Proceeds from the sales would be added to her RRSP, build her non-RRSP savings, and contribute to her child's savings. Roberta realized that tax would be due on these exercises and sales, but accepted this as the trade-off for a balanced investment portfolio.

STRATEGY #22

Evaluate Index-Linked GICs for Your Investment Strategy

More and more institutions are offering *index*-linked *GICs* for investors looking for more than the currently low returns available from traditional GICs. *Tax-smart* investors will notice that index-linked GICs may not be very attractive when owned outside an *RRSP* or *RRIF*. Here are some useful facts about these new products.

What Are Index-Linked GICs?

Index-linked GICs are investment products that combine the safety of a guaranteed investment certificate (GIC) with the investment return potential of an *equity* investment. An investor purchases a $5,000 GIC, for example, and receives a promise from the institution to get back at least the $5,000 at the end of the investment term. The potential rate of return on the GIC depends on the broader stock market index to which the GIC is tied (or linked). The extent to which the investor can earn the rate of return of the index (such as the TSE 100 index) will be set by the institution.

There are many varieties of index-linked GICs available.

They offer rates of return up to the potential returns of such indices as the TSE 100, S&P 500 in the U.S., and other internationally recognized indices.

What Are the Advantages of Index-Linked GICs?

• Index-linked GICs allow investors to share in the upside of the stock market without taking on the risk of owning an equity investment. In recent times of low-interest GICs, this potential for higher returns has become attractive.

• The taxation of an index-linked GIC is usually deferred until the maturity of the investment. This is because the amount of the return on the investment will not be known until maturity, when the institution calculates the rate of return based on the change in the linked index.

What Are the Disadvantages of Index-Linked GICs?

• Many of the index-linked GICs available provide only a portion of the upside of the stock market. For example, if the TSE 100 does 30% next year, investors may get only 20%. Other products provide the average return over a period of time. Investigate the specific product at the institution you deal with, to understand the limitations.

• Index-linked GICs are *tax disadvantaged*. Since the potential return is only "index linked" and not an actual investment in an index investment, investors do not receive any of the *dividends* paid by the corporations in the indices. Receiving dividends, which are taxed at a much lower rate than *interest*, would be desirable to taxable investors. Dividends can also rise over time, providing a basic *inflation* fighter to an otherwise fixed income. Additionally, the return from the index link is taxed as *regular income* instead of as tax-advantaged *capital gains* — as would be the case with a real index investment.

- There is some investment risk associated with an index-linked GIC, since when the investment matures you may receive only your original $5,000 principal back. No return may be guaranteed — as would be the case with a traditional GIC. And receiving no return means you've actually lost on your investment when you take inflation into account.

- The investment is a locked-in GIC which is not accessible until maturity. This does not provide flexibility.

- If the GIC permits you to look into a return during the term — say 20%, once the linked index reaches this level — you will be taxed on the accrued income when you lock in, even though you can't access the funds until maturity.

Who Are Index-Linked GICs Best Suited For?

These investments are more risky than traditional GICs (since no return may be guaranteed), but less risky than an outright investment in the stock market. They are suited for investors who want more potential return than GICs can offer, who can handle a bit of risk, but who aren't ready to deal with the potential loss of principal that could result from a direct investment in the stock market. Index-linked GICs are not suitable for someone who needs to live off annual income from the investment.

An investor's time frame is a key factor in deciding on these investments. Judging from history, investors will likely do better over the long term with a direct investment in the stock market than with an index-linked GIC. And why not receive tax-friendly dividends and capital gains instead of regular income? But in a short period of time (less than five years), the index-linked GIC may be more appropriate. If, for example, a couple are saving to buy a home in three years, they cannot afford a large drop in the stock market right before they plan to buy their home. Owning an index-linked GIC would prevent this from happening. But note that a zero return is also possible using index-linked GICs, if the stock market doesn't perform well.

Many elderly investors may be attracted to index-linked GICs because of the larger return potential. But buying an index-linked GIC (as a step toward investing in equities) should not be a substitute for appropriate *asset allocation* based on an analysis of *risk/return* for an investor. It may be more appropriate for seniors to invest their money in a 90% fixed income/10% equity *portfolio* that gives them tax advantages and inflation-fighting dividends than to buy an index-linked GIC that provides neither. And those seniors who need some investment income from their GICs should be aware that index-linked GICs may provide none at all if the stock market doesn't perform.

Example 1

Antonio and Mary were recently married and want to use the cash gifts they received at their wedding to save for their first home. With their $35,000, they have enough for the initial deposit, but they want to make a larger deposit in order to reduce the mortgage. They expect to buy in about five years, and would like to invest the $35,000 in an investment that can only grow. In other words, they want protection of the $35,000, but they also want the ability to make more money.

Antonio and Mary met with their financial advisor, who explained to the couple that an index-linked GIC could be the appropriate type of investment for them at this stage: it would provide a guarantee of their existing capital, but with the upside potential to earn a double-digit stock market return, since the return of the GIC would be linked to the return of the S&P 500 Index in the United States. With a guarantee of principal, Antonio and Mary could rest assured that if the stock market dropped the day before they needed their money, their original $35,000 wouldn't be affected. Antonio and Mary also liked the fact that the investment would be locked in for five years, preventing them from spending the money on less important but tempting items in the meantime.

▼

Example 2

Ivan and his wife of 50 years, Katarina, were finding it harder and harder to live on their fixed incomes in their retirement. With interest rates so low lately, their investment income was far less than it was five years ago. All of their savings were invested in short-term GICs. On top of that, rising inflation continued to erode their purchasing power, so that their cash flow was buying less and less.

Although they were risk-averse investors, Ivan and Katarina went to their local financial institutions in search of new investments to increase their returns. An advisor introduced them to index-linked GICs and discussed how they offered the potential for above-average returns with no additional risk.

Ivan and Katarina listened closely, and then, armed with a handful of brochures, they decided to seek a second opinion about these investments. They proceeded to visit their other financial institution, and sat down with a second advisor. "Oh, but they do come with risk," the advisor said. "The two of you require an annual income from your GICs, so just getting a guarantee of principal is useless. You need an annual income, and because many index-linked GICs don't offer this feature, they are not the right type of investment for you.

"Instead, your GICs should be part of a more balanced port-folio of investments. Around your GICs we should build a portfolio of investments that includes *bonds* and bond mutual funds and some equities or *equity mutual funds.* Because of your risk averseness and inexperience with the investment marketplace, perhaps the level of equities in your portfolio should be 25% or less overall. But even with this small amount, you will get exposure to the stock market and have the possibility of earning significant returns. The dividends and capital gains earned from the equity investments will provide tax-advantaged income as compared to interest. The bonds and bond funds will generate annual interest income and are not locked in like a GIC. That means you can access your money whenever you want."

After the advisor took much more time to fully explain his recommendations, Ivan and Katarina agreed with his logic. They did need annual income. And their aversion to risk didn't mean that they couldn't handle a small amount of equity in their portfolio. Exactly how much equity would always be under their control, and that put them more at ease.

STRATEGY #23

Acquire Short-Term Investments to Mature After December 31

This is an easy way to defer paying tax on an investment for an entire year. If you are purchasing *bonds* or *GICs* outside an *RRSP* or *RRIF* and the maturity date will fall late in the year, pick investments that last a few days or months longer and will mature in the new year. *Interest* income is generally taxable annually and on maturity of the investment, under the *Income Tax Act of Canada*. The last interest payment will fall on maturity of the investment. By having the maturity fall at the beginning of the next year, you can defer paying tax on the income until the following tax season — another year away.

A similar rule applies for *stock* investments. Rather than sell a stock in December and face taxation immediately on any *capital gains* realized, wait until January to sell the stock and defer paying tax on the gain for a whole year.

Obviously, these strategies must accommodate your need for the money and should be balanced with sound investment decisions. If, for example, you must sell late in the year because you need cash, the tax impact may become less important.

▼

Example

Susan owns several GICs in her *non-registered investment* portfolio. She has been in the habit of renewing one of these GICs every three months. Susan is waiting for interest rates to rise before she will buy a longer-term GIC. Meanwhile, she regularly receives an interest cheque from her financial institution for the earnings from the GICs, and she unhappily pays the income tax on these earnings each year.

It's now September, and Susan uses some new *tax-smart* investing knowledge and decides to purchase a four-month GIC instead of a three-month one on September 15 of the current year. The three-month GIC would have matured on December 15 of the current year and resulted in tax due on the income, but the new four-month GIC will mature in January, effectively deferring taxation of income earned on the four-month GIC for an entire year.

Deferring taxation of the GIC interest to the next year permits Susan to hold on to her money for the tax payment for an extra year, just by extending the maturity date by a month. Susan's GIC is large, and the tax deferral will be significant to her. Paying tax later means she will be able to invest the investment income for a longer time before having to pay tax on the income. This will generate even more income, which wouldn't have been possible if the income was needed this year to pay the tax bill.

STRATEGY #24

Invest Carefully Outside Canada

I am one of the first people to sing the praises of investing outside Canada. Not because Canada is a bad place in which to invest, but because Canada *could* be a bad place in which to invest, every once in a while. Global *diversification* can help to minimize the potential loss to your *portfolio* when a particular country is experiencing an economic downturn and poor economic performance. If Canada has a bad year, and you have invested in Canada, France, the United States, England, Australia, and Japan, then perhaps some of the other countries are having a good year, which will offset your Canadian losses. If you have invested only in Canada, however, you don't even have this chance.

There are tax disadvantages to investing outside Canada, though, and they relate to *dividends* in particular. Dividends received from Canadian *corporations* are one of the lowest-taxed types of investment income in Canada, and dividend-producing investments can play a role in many investors' portfolios. However, dividends received from non-Canadian corporations are not subject to the same *tax-advantaged* treatment as Canadian-source dividends. Instead, these foreign dividends are taxed as *regular income* — a big difference! That means you must purchase qualifying Canadian investments in order to take advantage of the preferential tax treatment available in Canada on dividend income. Whether they are from direct ownership in foreign stocks or ownership in international dividend funds, dividends are taxed as regular income if they are being received directly from non-Canadian companies.

Bearing this in mind, outside your *RRSP* or *RRIF* you should balance your global investing with some Canadian *equity* investments that pay Canadian dividends. This will ensure that you get some favourable tax treatment from earning Canadian dividends and reduce your tax bill on investment income.

An additional tip: some companies in Canada offer dividend-paying preferred shares denominated in foreign currencies (like U.S. dollars). This type of investment may permit you to access the lower taxation of Canadian-source dividends and still achieve global diversification by purchasing a foreign-currency investment. Diversification of investments across markets, currencies, and investment types can reduce your *investment risk.*

▼

Example

Barbara knew that dividend income is taxed in a preferential manner in Canada and she wanted to take advantage of this. Inside her RRSP she was holding several *international equity mutual funds,* which were generating dividends that were being categorized as *foreign income* for tax purposes. Barbara smiled because she knew that inside her RRSP, where taxation of investment income didn't matter, this income tax treatment on foreign investments had no impact. She wasn't being *tax disadvantaged,* and she was maximizing her *foreign content* through ownership of international investments.

However, outside her RRSP she had bought a few units of the same fund. Barbara knew that while she was getting international exposure, she was losing the war on tax, since the foreign dividends were not being taxed at the lower rate applicable to Canadian dividends. Instead, the foreign dividends were being classified as foreign income as noted on her mutual fund *T3 tax slip* last year.

With help from her advisor, Barbara decided not to sell these non-RRSP investments, because while they had appreciated nicely, the amount was small and to sell them would attract tax and additional transaction fees that would take several years to recover through tax savings from new Canadian investments generating Canadian dividends.

Instead, in the future Barbara would try to be more aware of the source of dividend-producing investments, and she would select some Canadian dividend-generating investments to take advantage of the favourable tax rates applicable to these dividends. International diversification would continue to be addressed through her RRSP and with some of her non-RRSP investments.

Crunching the Numbers

Barbara's current fund investment:

LOQ International Equity Fund generated the following income and gains last year:

Interest	$300
Capital gains	$250
Foreign income	$1,250

Total tax paid by Barbara (highest marginal rate):

$300 x 50%
$250 x 38%
$1,250 x 50%   **Total tax bill $870**

If Barbara was to convert the foreign income to Canadian dividend income by investing in a different equity fund, her tax savings could be $1,250 x (50% – 34%) = $200 every year.

STRATEGY #25

Utilize a Buy-and-Hold Investment Strategy to Defer Paying Tax

This strategy is all about controlling *asset turnover* on *equity* investments. The easiest way to avoid paying taxes in the short term is to delay the sale of any investments with *accrued capital gains* and to buy *equity mutual fund*s that don't frequently sell the investments held inside those funds. As long as investments such as *stocks* or equity *mutual funds* are not sold by you, and the *fund managers* running the funds also *buy and hold* for longer periods of time, your investments can continue to appreciate in value without attracting immediate tax on the accruing capital gains. There will be tax to pay on any *dividends* distributed to you, but there is no taxation on capital gains until a *disposition* occurs. It's a simple "buy-and-hold" strategy.

This type of strategy may not be desirable with non-*RRSP/RRIF* money where the funds are being saved for a specific short-term purpose and the intent is to dispose of the investments shortly. And bear in mind that this strategy is only a *deferral of tax*. Someday there will be a disposition or *deemed disposition* of this investment, when tax will be due on the capital gain realized. But in the meantime, next to a *tax deduction*, a tax deferral is the next best thing for the average Canadian trying to keep his or her tax bill low. Of course, it is an added benefit if you are in a lower tax bracket when you eventually sell the investments with the accrued gains (perhaps in retirement) and pay less tax overall on the investments than you might today.

This buy-and-hold strategy may work better for individual stocks than for mutual funds. Actively trading mutual fund managers will generate distributions of *interest*, dividends, and capital gains that are taxable. As an owner of an actively traded fund, you have no control over the generation of capital gains from the manager's buying and selling. All you can do is purchase funds that have a value-focused investing policy — that is, the manager's policy is to buy and hold. This type of fund will have reduced *asset* turnover, resulting in more deferred capital gains. You will continue to receive dividends and interest, though, since this type of income is not affected by turnover.

So when holding investments that appreciate in value, and where those increases will be taxed as capital gains, consider keeping the investments for longer periods. If you delay paying the tax on the capital gains, your investment capital is maximized and working for you. In terms of growing your *net worth*, the longer you can practise this strategy, the more net worth you should have over time, even after the tax is eventually paid.

▼

Example

Donna purchased 1,000 *shares* of the *common stock* of XYZ Bank as a long-term investment to add to her existing portfolio of GICs. Donna plans to sell both investments in the next eight years and use the proceeds to purchase a cottage.

A year after the stock purchase, Donna decided to purchase a new car and wanted to pay for the car using some of her invested funds. Since the stock purchase last year, the bank stock had appreciated nicely and was paying regular dividends to Donna as well. Using a *tax-smart* investing strategy, Donna waited for the *GICs* to mature and used the proceeds to purchase the vehicle. The GICs attracted no taxation other than the tax on the interest income she received.

By using the GIC proceeds instead of selling the bank stock to fund her cash need, Donna actually followed two tax-smart investing strategies: first, she avoided realizing a capital gain from the bank shares and paying the related tax; and second, she sold the investment that was producing the *higher-tax-rate income* — interest income is taxed at higher *marginal tax rates* than dividends. Rather than rushing out and selling any old investment to buy the car, Donna had thought about the tax consequences and minimized her tax bill this year.

Crunching the Numbers

Donna's successful buy-and-hold strategy

1,000 shares at $100/share, for a total cost of $100,000. Assuming a 12% growth rate annually, compounded, and excluding the impact of the dividends, this investment will be worth close to $248,000 at the end of eight years. At a tax rate of 38% for capital gains, Donna will pay $56,240 in tax — ($248K – $100K) x 38%. This will leave her with after-tax cash of $191,760 for the cottage.

Had Donna bought and sold more frequently

Now suppose Donna had made the same investments under the same conditions, but sold the shares at the end of the fourth year and reinvested the after-tax proceeds for the remaining four years.

At the end of year four, the proceeds would be $157,300 less cost of $100,000 for a gain of $57,300. Tax at 38% would be $21,770, and the reinvestment amount would be $157,300 less $21,770, or $135,530.

That $135,530 invested for the next four years, again with a 12% return, would produce proceeds of $213,300. Cost would now be $135,530; the gain would be $77,770. Tax at 38% on the gain would be $29,550, to produce after-tax cash flow of $213,300 less $29,550 or $183,750.

Thus, the pure buy-and-hold strategy Donna selected generated close to $8,000 more in the end. This difference would be even greater if more buying and selling occurred in the second option.

STRATEGY #26

Invest to Fight Inflation

Inflation is a term representing the increase in cost of living over time. Examples of the impact of inflation have been the rising cost of postage stamps, automobiles, and homes over the years. As the cost of living increases because of inflation, your income must also grow at the same pace in order to prevent a decrease in your standard of living.

When an individual buys a fixed income investment like a *GIC*, a rate of return is locked in for a period of time. During this same period of time, however, inflation continues to eat into *purchasing power*. For example, assume a GIC earning 6% annually is taxed at approximately 50% (for a Canadian in the top marginal tax bracket). This means that the after-tax return is only 3%. However, suppose that inflation in the same year is 3.5%. This means that the real rate of return on the GIC is – 0.5%. In other words, the investor lost ground. For people purchasing fixed income investments, this scenario is a real possibility.

There are, however, investments available that can fight inflation. Three examples are *dividend*-paying investments, rental properties, and indexed *bonds* (or real return bonds). Dividend income is generated by investment in *stocks* that pay dividends to shareholders. *Mutual funds* that invest in stocks may also pay dividend income. Many public companies, especially large *blue-chip* companies, pay dividends to their shareholders. Additionally, companies may regularly increase their dividend payments to shareholders. Many companies have long histories of raising dividend amounts. Raising dividend amounts is important because it offsets some or all of annual inflation and helps shareholders keep pace with the rising cost of living.

Rental income is the net profit that arises from owning a rental property or units in a *real estate investment trust.* (Real estate investment trusts are discussed in Strategy #14.) Rental income is a good inflation fighter since the income is derived from rents that people pay when they rent accommodations owned by an individual or a real estate investment trust. These rents generally increase over time (perhaps subject to rent controls) and thus an investor may receive an increasing amount of rent which keeps pace with inflation. In addition, the value of the property may increase with inflation.

Indexed bonds are bond investments where the rate of return is regularly adjusted for an inflation factor.

From a tax point of view, rental properties and bonds generate *regular income* and *interest* income respectively, which are taxed at the least favourable rate in Canada. (A *capital gain* may also occur on the eventual sale of the investments, which would have a more favourable tax treatment.) Dividends are more favourably taxed and may be more desirable from a pure tax point of view.

Consider purchasing these types of investments as part of a well-balanced investment *portfolio.* Holding these type of assets can help you keep pace with inflation and guard against a decrease in your standard of living.

▼

Example

Dan is 65 and has been retired for 10 years already. He and his wife are living on his fixed pension, some *non-registered* investments, and an *RRSP* in his wife's name that they haven't drawn on yet. In his 10 years of retirement, Dan has already noticed that he and his wife are finding it harder to stretch a dollar. He has realized that his fixed pension is buying less and less every year as inflation raises the cost of basic goods and services. Even something as basic as the cost of riding the bus seems to be growing out of control.

Dan has been doing his own investing, and all of his portfolio is conservatively invested in GICs. Dan has never really thought about investing in anything else, but thinks there must be more out there in terms of investments that will cost less in tax and increase his cash flow.

Recently, Dan's son introduced him to an investment advisor, Emma. Emma reviewed Dan's portfolio and noticed the fixed income investments. Appreciating his desire for low risk, Emma suggested that Dan take a small portion of his non-RRSP portfolio and purchase a good-quality, low-cost *blue-chip* dividend mutual fund. Dan agreed to part with an amount of money that he felt he could comfortably invest in the stock market, and permitted Emma to make the purchase on his behalf. Dan was committed for a five-year trial.

A year later, when Dan went to prepare his tax return, he noticed that some of his interest income was replaced this year with dividend income. He also noticed that his tax bill had shrunk in size, and he wondered why. He called Emma and she explained that dividend income is taxed at a much lower rate than interest income. Dan was pleased.

Some time after Dan filed his tax return, he noticed that the mutual fund distributions were getting slightly larger. He asked Emma why this was happening. She told him that sometimes the corporations paying the dividends raise the dividends for a variety of reasons. She pointed out that many of the largest *corporations* have a long history of regularly raising dividends. These increases in dividends serve as a good inflation fighter to keep an individual's income rising with the cost of living, and would help Dan to be able to afford the rising cost of taking the bus.

Why Does a Dividend Fund Need to Be Low-Cost?

Dividends generated by investments in Canada typically amount to only a few percent of return each year. The return is enhanced by the favourable tax treatment offered for dividends. (See Strategy #27 for more information.) But with a low dividend distribution, these amounts can quickly be eaten up by a mutual fund with high management expenses (a high *MER*). For this reason, pay attention to cost of fund management with dividend funds, or consider supplementing the dividend funds with some direct ownership in high-quality, high-dividend-yielding shares.

One concern with high-dividend-paying investments (like utilities stocks, for example) is that they can be particularly sensitive to interest-rate changes. While they are desirable as inflation fighters, in periods of rising interest rates their share price may decrease. Why might interest rates rise? One reason is rising inflation! Keep this in consideration when investigating dividend-generating investments.

STRATEGY #27

Convert Some of Your Interest Income to Dividend Income to Boost Cash Flow

Individuals who need a steady flow of cash to help pay the bills believe that a large tax bill is the price they have to pay for safe and reliable *interest* income. But have these individuals ever considered *dividend* income? There can be quite a large difference in after-tax returns between interest and dividend income. One must earn approximately $132 in interest income to produce the same amount of after-tax income as $100 of dividends. This means that a 4.5% dividend may produce the same after-tax return as roughly 6% in interest income.

And what about *inflation* considerations? Interest-bearing investments pay a fixed rate of interest. The purchasing power of this interest income is reduced over time by inflation. This means that while a 6% *GIC* after-tax may pay only 3% to an investor, if inflation for that year was 4% then the investor actually lost ground on the investment — a – 1% real return! — since his or her dollar has less *purchasing power*.

Investors, including seniors, should consider holding some high-dividend-yielding *stocks*, or dividend-generating *mutual funds* that invest in high-yielding dividend stocks. Because these stocks are income oriented, management of the companies may also try to increase dividends regularly. Rising dividends provide a hedge against inflation that regular *bonds* and GICs usually don't offer. As well, outside an *RRSP* or *RRIF* many Canadian dividend-generating investments can offer a great break on taxes.

Yes, purchasing stocks or stock mutual funds is more risky than buying GICs, but high-dividend-yielding stocks in Canada tend to be in utilities, resource companies, banks, and telephone companies. Several of these organizations are some of Canada's largest *corporations* and have a long history of paying dividends and increasing these dividends. To offset your concern about risk, purchase only an amount of stock or dividend-generating mutual funds that you are comfortable with, and that makes sense as part of a diversified portfolio.

As an added tax bonus, high-dividend-yielding stocks or dividend-generating mutual funds also offer the potential to earn *capital gains* from the increase in stock price owned directly or through the mutual fund. Capital gains, like dividends, are *tax advantaged* compared to interest. Of course, stocks can sometimes result in *capital losses* as well!

One last tip: Canadians can purchase dividend-yielding stocks that typically pay in Canadian dollars, but Canadian-sourced dividends payable in foreign currencies like U.S. dollars also exist. Purchasing some of these foreign-pay investments allows additional *diversification* from foreign-currency exposure. These investments, being Canadian sourced, may also qualify for the preferential tax treatment afforded to taxable Canadian dividends.

▼

Example

François is 60, has retired, and dislikes completing his income tax return each year. It seems as though he is always paying more and more tax. Even worse, his accountant just told him that because of the large amount of interest income he earned last year, he will have to start paying income tax instalments as well. François needed the interest income to live on, but he doesn't like paying the related tax on the income. He is in the highest tax bracket, and at his *marginal tax rate* of 50%, he is keeping only half of his interest income. François asked his accountant if there was any planning he could consider to help his situation.

His accountant explained the taxation of different types of investment income. François is particularly interested in the dividends, which at his marginal rate would be taxed at approximately 34% — much less than 50%. The accountant added that dividends would also fight inflation over time since dividends may be increased periodically by the company paying them.

The accountant referred François to a trusted and reliable investment advisor friend to learn more about dividends and to investigate dividend-paying investments. The investment advisor explained to François that he could create a *portfolio* of high-dividend-yielding stocks or he could purchase a dividend mutual fund. The investment advisor recommended the dividend fund because François didn't want to invest much money and many more companies can be invested in through a mutual fund when you have only a small amount of money to invest.

François could convert a small amount of his existing portfolio of interest-bearing GICs to dividend funds when the GICs mature, as a first step to replacing his interest income with dividend income. Over time, François might consider increasing this dividend-generating piece of his portfolio as he becomes more comfortable with dividends and dividend funds. Purchasing gradually over time would permit François to "test-drive" the products before buying them in any significant quantities and would keep his total investment portfolio at a level of risk he is comfortable with.

Crunching the Numbers

Current portfolio and taxes:

$2,000,000	in GICs
5%	return last year
$100,000	total income
50%	tax rate
$50,000	**tax paid**
$50,000	**disposable income left**

Future portfolio and taxes, including some dividend-producing investments:

$1,500,000	in GICs
$500,000	in conservative dividend-yielding funds or stocks
$2,000,000	total portfolio
4.75%	return last year (5% on GICs, 4% on dividends)
$95,000	total income
46.63%	tax rate (50% on interest, 34% on dividends)
$44,300	**tax paid**
$50,700	**disposable income left**

With this mix of investments, François could increase his annual disposable income by $700.

For additional advice on dividends, see Strategy #26.

STRATEGY #28

Contribute Equities as a Charitable Donation to Save Tax

Recently, the Minister of Finance has made significant improvements to the benefits related to charitable giving in Canada. Individuals are entitled to a non-refundable *tax credit* of 17% on the first $200 of donations, plus 29% on gifts made that are in excess of $200 (with even larger credits when you factor in related provincial tax credits). The maximum annual amount permissible for a tax credit is 75% of the individual's personal net income plus 25% of any *taxable capital gains* resulting from the charitable gifts and 25% of any *recapture* of *depreciation* arising from the donation of depreciable property such as an apartment block.

To encourage gifts of appreciated *assets*, the federal government recently reduced the income inclusion rate from 75% to 37.5% on *capital gains* arising from donations made after February 18, 1997, of certain property to charities. Eligible property includes *shares* of public companies, *bonds*, trust *units, mutual funds,* and some other investments. This means that if you make large charitable donations and also will sell investments to realize capital gains in the same year, you should consider giving the investments to a charity, to realize an overall tax saving.

And if you are deciding whether to contribute cash or mutual funds or another investment, consider your investment strategy before doing so. If you would otherwise hold a mutual fund that has grown in value as a long-term investment, a cash donation would likely be more tax effective. Donating the mutual fund would result in an early payment of tax on the mutual fund's accrued gain that otherwise could be deferred.

Here is another tip: remember how your federal tax credit is 17% on the first $200 of charitable donations, and then the credit rises to 29%? Well, it is in your best interest to try to get the 29% credit and achieve more tax-credit bang for your donation buck. Therefore, an individual and his or her spouse should consider claiming all their donations on one tax return each year, to ensure that they get over the $200 threshold. Couples currently claiming less than $200 on each of their tax returns may be losing out on an additional 12% federal tax credit (up to 20% combined federal-provincial) every year! You could also save donations for a few years in order to get over the threshold, because the donation credit is based on donations made in the current year and previous five years as long as the gifts haven't been claimed on a previous tax return.

Finally, consider timing your donations appropriately to take advantage of the higher tax credit. A $400 donation in one year compared to two $200 donations over two years can save you about $40.

▼

Example

Enzo lives a comfortable lifestyle and is thankful for all he has. He has a successful career, a wonderful family, and a large investment *portfolio*, which he created himself through active investing. He is a believer in giving back to the community that helped him, and is in the habit of making sizable charitable donations to several charities each year. In the past, Enzo just wrote a cheque at the end of each year for all of his charitable contributions. He never thought about mixing his charitable contributions with his investments before. Rather, he kept his investment portfolio separate: he actively bought *stocks* and bonds, and simply sold something when he needed funds to finance living expenses. At year end, when he made his donations, he usually sold some of his short-term investments to cover the cash requirement.

Recently, Enzo was talking to his new tax accountant, Katie, about tax-planning opportunities. Enzo hired Katie to do a complete review of his tax situation to see if any planning opportunities were possible. Enzo had been doing his own taxes, and thought an independent professional review made sense. Katie spent some time going over Enzo's situation, and reported that he should consider making his annual charitable donations using stocks, rather than selling the stocks first and then contributing cash. Katie also confirmed with Enzo that this would be sensible because a number of his stock investments were ripe for sale in any case.

Crunching the Numbers

Katie described the benefits of this strategy as follows:

	Sell stocks and donate cash	Donate stock
Stock market value at sale date	$11,000	$11,000
Tax cost	$1,000	$1,000
Capital gain realized	$10,000	$10,000
Taxable gain included in personal income for the year	$7,500	$3,750
Tax on taxable gain (assume 50%)	($3,750)	($1,875)
Tax benefit of donation ($11,000 x 50% assuming all high rate)	$5,500	$5,500
Net tax benefit (tax benefit from credit less tax paid)	$1,750	$3,625
Tax savings from direct stock donation		**$1,875**

By donating stock instead of cash, Enzo can reduce his tax bill every year that he follows this strategy. The tax savings result because only 37.5% of the capital gain from the donation is included in income, as compared to the 75% income inclusion when the stock is sold personally.

STRATEGY #29

Downsize Your Home in Retirement to Improve Your Cash Flow and Lifestyle

Here's something you may have seen: an elderly couple living on a small fixed pension and receiving some government benefits. They live a meagre fixed income lifestyle, getting by with few luxuries. This same couple is proud to state, however, that they own their home, the same home they've had for 40 years, and it is their pride and joy.

While there may be nothing wrong with this lifestyle, these seniors are *asset* rich and cash poor. Yes, they enjoy home ownership, but they may be sacrificing a more enjoyable day-to-day lifestyle in order to hang on to an oversized four-bedroom house. Keeping a large, valuable home because you "need the space when the kids visit one week a year" may mean you are giving up a lot in those other 51 weeks. This scenario is especially true in cities like Vancouver and Toronto where the value of homes has significantly increased in the last 30 years.

Seniors should consider *downsizing* their home as early as age 60. Downsizing may mean buying a smaller home, buying a condominium, or moving into an apartment, depending on personal preferences. If downsizing frees up even $100,000, this amount earning a basic 5% pre-tax can result in another $3,000 or so to the senior's after-tax income every year. That's a lot of money to seniors living on a small fixed income, and that money could enhance their lifestyle — maybe even pay for a vacation to see the kids!

Another nice thing about downsizing is that many of the things you enjoy about owning a home don't have to change if you simply buy a smaller home. But the boost to your cash flow will add to your daily lifestyle year after year.

This strategy can be applied to other valuable assets you own as a senior, such as antiques, art, or collectible stamps, for example. If you would love to visit your relatives across Canada every year but really can't afford it, consider selling the cottage you only use on long weekends and using the income from the invested proceeds to travel. You can always rent another cottage for a few weeks a year.

Take a long hard look at the assets you own as a senior, and determine if there are better uses for your money.

▼

Example

When Roger and Marg retired 10 years ago, they knew their fixed income pensions might force them to change their lifestyle. Since then, they have managed to fit their lifestyle into their income of $40,000 a year. But in the decade they have been retired, they have already noticed the impact that *inflation* has had on their standard of living. Their pensions are buying less and less each year.

Roger and Marg are hoping they can use their $190,000 in *RRIFs* to offset the inflation loss. With both of them at age 70 now, they realize this money may have to last another 25 years. With their home in Toronto paid off and no other debt, they think they can make it. They believe they'll just have to watch their spending.

When some of Roger's RRIF investments came due recently, they sat down with their *financial planner*, Chuck. He knows the financial situation of Roger and Marg well, and has already helped them to fight inflation by guiding them to buy some *dividend*-generating investments.

In their recent meeting, Chuck decided to make another suggestion. Roger and Marg would probably squeeze by financially in retirement, but they would never have the extra cash to enjoy a few more vacations, buy a new car, or even give a bit of money to their grandchildren. Chuck pointed out that the home Roger and Marg lived in was worth $380,000, growing at about 1% annually, and providing no income. Downsizing to a smaller home or condo could permit $200,000 to be invested, which could produce annual before-tax income of $10,000 at a 5% rate of return. Cash flow for Marg and Roger could be even higher when the savings from lower property taxes and utilities are included. And because the home is their principal residence, the large *capital gain* realized on the sale would not be taxable!

Chuck also suggested that if Roger and Marg were prepared to rent, the full net-sale proceeds could be invested; this action could potentially cause their total family income to grow by 50% (pre-tax) from its current level, every year.

Roger and Marg were cool to the idea. They said their home was their castle and leaving it wouldn't be easy. But vacations and being able to afford pleasures like more golf were also important. They realized there was no rush to act, so they promised Chuck they would consider it.

STRATEGY #30

Monitor Your U.S. Investment Position

The *performance* of U.S. *equity* markets over the past few years has been superb and, as a result, many Canadian investors have built up significant holdings in U.S. securities. While reveling in their successes, these investors likely don't realize they may be creating an exposure to U.S. *estate* tax.

Unlike Canada, the U.S. imposes a gift tax and an estate tax. If an individual is a resident of the United States or a U.S. citizen, the estate tax is applied to all *assets* owned at the time of death. However, even where an individual is neither a citizen nor a resident of the United States, U.S. estate tax may be levied on the value of certain property, known as "U.S. *situs*" property, owned at the time of death. The rate of this tax ranges between 18% and 55%, increasing as the value of the estate increases.

The type of property that a Canadian might own that may be subject to U.S. estate tax includes: real estate and personal property situated in the United States, *shares* of U.S. *corporations,* and debt obligations issued by U.S. residents, like *bonds* or debentures. U.S. securities held in registered plans, such as *RRSPs* and *RRIFs* may also be considered U.S. *situs* property. However, cash deposits in U.S. bank accounts are not. This doesn't mean that all Canadians who own U.S. *stocks* have to be worried about U.S. estate tax. If the value of your worldwide estate at the time of death is less than $1.2 million US, the estate tax will apply only to real property, resource property, and business property situated in the U.S. So, if the only U.S. property you own is shares of U.S. companies (other than those whose assets are principally U.S. real estate) and bonds, there will be no U.S. estate tax exposure if your worldwide assets are worth less than $1.2 million US.

However, even if an individual's estate exceeds $1.2 million US, there are some tax-relief measures available under the Canada–U.S. tax treaty to reduce a potential U.S. estate tax liability. These include:

- An exemption on the first $625,000 US of U.S. assets, but this exemption must be prorated based on the proportion of the value of U.S. assets in the estate to the total value of all assets in the estate. So if, for example, your U.S. investments represent 10% of the value of all assets owned at the time of death, the exemption will be only $62,500 US.
- An additional marital credit against the estate tax where the property is left to the Canadian individual's spouse or a spousal *trust*.
- A credit against Canadian income tax payable in the year of death that is related to the U.S. property (this will generally be the Canadian tax that results from the *deemed disposition* of assets at *fair market value*), subject to the Canadian foreign *tax credit* rules and limitations for any remaining U.S. estate tax after the first two credits.

Even with these exemptions and credits, on death, the total tax payable relating to U.S. assets (combined Canadian and

U.S. tax) may be greater than the Canadian tax that would have been payable had the assets been Canadian property. You will not necessarily avoid U.S. estate tax through *joint ownership* of assets. In general, where property is owned jointly with another person, the first to die will be presumed to own the entire property unless it can be proved that the joint owner also contributed to the purchase price of the property with his or her own funds. The value of jointly owned property included in a deceased's estate will be in proportion to that person's contribution to its cost. There are certain exceptions to this rule.

So, if you own significant U.S. investments and perhaps real estate in the United States, assess your exposure to U.S. estate tax and, if that exposure is high, take steps to minimize it. Selling the U.S. investments before death would work, but doesn't take into account accidental deaths. Adequate insurance could be used to pay U.S. estate tax, or you might consider using a Canadian corporation to hold U.S. securities. In any case, if you believe you may be exposed, consult a professional tax advisor to help you develop an effective plan.

▼

Example

Belinda, a single mother of two, is a senior programmer for the Canadian subsidiary of a large, successful public U.S. software company. She has been with the company for over ten years, and within that time period she has acquired a significant number of shares of the company through *stock options* and market purchases. Believing that the high-tech industry will continue to grow, she has also invested in shares of a number of other U.S. computer companies. She estimates that her current holdings in U.S. securities are worth approximately $750,000.

One evening, Belinda went out for dinner with an old friend from university, who happened to be a tax accountant. The conversation turned to the stock market and Belinda was eager to talk about her investment successes. She told Monty that she had managed to accumulate a *net worth* of about $750,000 by investing in high-tech U.S. stocks and she expected this to increase significantly over the next ten years.

Although Monty didn't like talking business when out with friends, he felt compelled to ask Belinda whether she was aware of the possible U.S. estate tax implications if her investment *portfolio* increased in value. Belinda was somewhat surprised. She had never lived in the U.S., so why would U.S. estate tax be an issue? Monty briefly explained the rules and suggested that she consult with one of his partners who was a *financial planner*.

Belinda met with Sophie the next week. Sophie explained that based on Belinda's current assets there was no U.S. estate tax exposure; however, if she continued to invest in U.S. equities or if the shares she currently owned appreciated in value significantly, there might be U.S. estate tax exposure. Sophie also pointed out that there was virtually no *diversification* in Belinda's portfolio. If the high-tech market took a downturn, Belinda's net worth could tumble. This made Belinda very nervous, particularly since she was financially responsible for two children and wanted to ensure that they would be well provided for in the case of her death.

After a careful analysis of Belinda's current financial position, Sophie recommended that Belinda sell some of her high-tech stock and invest in other industry sectors and other countries, using high-quality *mutual funds*. Although this would result in some immediate tax, it was less risky in the long term.

Belinda was grateful for the advice. Although she intended to continue to invest some of her money in the high-tech sector because she thought it would continue to do well, she realized the importance of protecting her net worth. She agreed to meet with Sophie annually to monitor her position in relation to U.S. estate tax and her financial goals in general.

STRATEGY #31

Buy Assets from Your Spouse

Tax-smart investing can sometimes be achieved very effectively in simple ways. This strategy is a good example. Many families have only one spouse earning income that is being taxed in the highest tax bracket, at approximately 50%. The other spouse may have little or no income. Unfortunately, due to the *attribution rules* in the *Income Tax Act*, the higher-earning spouse cannot gift money to the other spouse to invest and have the other spouse pay tax on the investment income at a lower tax rate. Because of these attribution rules, the income earned on the transferred funds is attributed back to the higher-earning spouse and taxed in his or her hands. Nevertheless, when one spouse has a much lower *marginal tax rate*, the desired goal is to move some of the highly taxed investment income of the higher-earning spouse into the hands of the lower-taxed spouse.

A tax-smart investing strategy to accomplish this objective is available when the lower-earning spouse owns some valuable assets, either completely or partially. If, for example,·the lower-earning spouse inherited a cottage from his or her parents, or inherited some valuable antiques, or used some of his or her own income to purchase part of the family home or cottage, there may be an opportunity to save tax. The key is that the lower earner must be the property owner; that is, this person inherited the *asset* or used his or her own funds to buy the asset.

The lower-income spouse could sell this valuable asset (e.g., the cottage) or share of an asset (e.g., half of the family home) to the higher-earning spouse for *fair market value.* Note that any accrued gain on the property sold to the spouse will be taxed (unless the home is a principal residence), and this tax cost should be considered in determining the overall economic benefit of the transaction. Also, in order for the transaction to take place at fair market value for tax purposes, the couple will have to elect out of the automatic transfer that occurs at cost, for tax purposes, between spouses. This transaction will permit the higher-earning spouse to transfer investable wealth (as payment for the asset) to the lower-earning spouse *without* triggering the attribution rules of the Income Tax Act. The lower-earning spouse can then invest the proceeds received from the sale and pay tax on the related investment income at a lower tax rate than the higher-earning spouse would on earning that income. This means that instead of a potential 50% tax rate on the resulting investment, a much smaller tax rate would apply. In fact, there will be no tax at all on the first several thousand dollars of investment income if the lower-earning spouse has no other income. Moreover, the couple will save this amount every year that income continues to be generated on the invested funds and taxed in the lower-earning spouse's hands.

Note, however, that the resulting taxable income in the lower-earning spouse's hands will reduce or eliminate the married exemption *tax credit.*

▼

Example

Mae earns a salary of $100,000 and investment income of approximately $24,000. She pays tax at a marginal rate of 50%. Her husband, Jim, makes $22,000 a year and has a marginal tax rate of 27%. Jim's last surviving parent passed away recently and Jim inherited the family cottage worth $300,000. In order to take advantage of tax-smart investing, Jim and Mae decided he should immediately sell the cottage to Mae.

Mae verified that the legal costs and land transfer taxes associated with the sale of the cottage were immaterial compared to the tax savings involved. The transaction was formalized by their lawyer and approved by their accountant shortly after. Jim and Mae consulted their tax accountant to ensure that the appropriate tax elections were made such that the attribution rules would not apply to the transaction. Mae sold off some of her non-*RRSP* investment portfolio in order to buy the cottage, being careful to sell investments that didn't trigger any *taxable capital gains*, by selling some of her *Treasury bills* instead of her *stocks*. (Mae could have sold her investments directly to Jim in exchange for the cottage.)

Upon receiving the cheque from Mae, Jim invested the proceeds into a balanced investment portfolio consisting of *equity mutual funds, bonds,* and Treasury bills. This transaction shifted approximately $24,000 of annual investment income (historical income, which may not be as high in the future!) into Jim's hands for tax purposes, and will save approximately $3,000 in taxes every year that the money is invested.

Crunching the Numbers

Before the sale: $300,000 worth of investments owned by Mae earning 8% would generate approximately $24,000 of investment income annually. Mae would pay approximately 50% tax on this income and keep only $12,000 after-tax.

After the sale (ignoring non-income tax consequences such as professional fees and any land transfer taxes): $300,000 worth of investments are now owned by Jim, who has invested them and expects to earn an 8% rate of return annually. Jim will pay approximately 27% in tax on $8,000 and 43% on $16,000 of the investment income, or total tax of $9,040 on the $24,000 of investment income. Jim and the family will now keep $14,960 ($24,000 less $9,040) of income after-tax every year, for an increase of $2,960 annually.

STRATEGY #32

Gift Money to Your Adult Children

If you meet a few criteria, you should consider gifting money to your adult children. (Adult children are children aged 18 or older.) The criteria are as follows:

- You can afford to part with the money permanently, and wish to help out your children with various expenditures in the future;
- You believe that your children have the financial common sense to use the money wisely and also have a need for the money;
- You are not concerned about your children's marital situations or the possibility of their personal *bankruptcy*.

Gifting can have significant tax advantages. If you are in the highest *tax bracket* in Canada and are paying tax at approximately 50%, gifting cash to adult children in lower tax brackets can have several benefits:

- If you use the gift to start an *RRSP* for your adult children, the RRSP investment eliminates all current tax on the investment (since it is now tax sheltered) and will save all of the tax you would otherwise pay on investment income.

- If the gift is used to pay off a mortgage, your adult children will be able to reduce or eliminate paying non-tax-deductible *interest* costs out of their disposable income. This means that gifting them $1,000 costs you $30 in interest ($1,000 gift x 6% interest you could have earned x 50% tax rate). On the other hand, the gift saves the children $80 ($1,000 mortgage reduction x 8% mortgage interest rate) they would otherwise be paying on the mortgage. That's a net $50 improvement to the family.

- Even if the adult children just invest the gift, tax will be saved by the family overall if their *marginal tax rates* are lower than yours.

- The gift can be used to pay for post-secondary education.

Example

Ivy decided she wanted to start her son Billy off right by making the initial contribution to a new RRSP for him. Billy is 20, in university, and (like most students) short on cash, especially to invest. Since age 15, however, Billy had been filing tax returns to report his summer job income, and he had accumulated RRSP contribution room of $4,800.

Ivy made a $4,800 RRSP contribution for Billy in 1997 and by doing so accomplished several *tax-smart* investing goals:

- She reduced the tax she was paying on the investment earnings from 50% to 0% inside Billy's RRSP (although RRSP savings are only a tax deferral).

- She started Billy's RRSP 10 to 20 years earlier than any-one his age might. Due to the power of compounding for the next 60 years, Billy should have a large head start on his retirement plan.
- She made the contribution for Billy but he did not take the tax deduction. Instead, he is saving the tax deduction until after he graduates and has a higher income level. At that time, the deduction can be applied against income that would be taxed in a higher tax bracket, and this will result in a larger tax refund to Billy.

Crunching the Numbers

The RRSP contribution of $4,800, growing at 8% a year and compounded for 60 years, will amount to $486,000. Had Ivy not made the contribution, and Billy had instead made the contribution in 10 years' time when he had sufficient funds, that same amount, growing at 8% a year but compounded for only 50 years, would amount to $225,000. That's a difference of $261,000. Clearly, it pays to start early!

STRATEGY #33

Beware Informal In-Trust Accounts for Children's Savings

Many financial advisors are advising parents to set up a *mutual fund* account earning *capital gains* "in trust" for their children, as a savings vehicle for the children. Under the *Income Tax Act*'s *attribution rules*, capital gains earned by a child under age 18 are taxable in the child's hands, not those of the parents who provided the funds for the investment. While this plan appears to produce effective family income-splitting by taxing the capital gains in the child's hands, it may not be that easy. There is a risk that the "in-trust" account will fail to meet Revenue Canada's standards, resulting in the parents being re-assessed and having to pay tax on the capital gains earned in the *trust* account. Note that a parent, as contributor, will already have to pay tax on any *interest* or *dividends* earned.

The first critical question is, does the in-trust account actually form a trust for tax purposes? To qualify, there must be clear identification of the *trustee*, the trust contributor or settlor, and the *beneficiaries*. If the account is titled "Mrs. X in trust for Tommy" and the funds are contributed by Mr. X, the test should be met. It is clear that the mother is the trustee and the child is the beneficiary. Mr. X is the settlor. But an account opened as "Mrs. X in trust" doesn't meet the Revenue Canada test, because the beneficiaries are not named.

Second, has a transfer of funds or investments to the trust actually occurred? Revenue Canada says the settlor or trust contributor cannot also be the trustee. So Mr. and Mrs. X should agree that one spouse will provide the funding to the trust and the other spouse will be the trustee. The trustee is solely responsible for the ongoing operation of the trust and the investment decision-making inside the trust. The contributor parent must give up all control of the transferred funds, so that funds or assets cannot revert back to the contributing parent.

Take note: should Revenue Canada decide to declare an in-trust account not to be a valid trust, all of the capital gains from such an account would be taxable back to the contributor.

With an *informal trust*, other concerns may include issues like divorce of the parents, sudden death of the parents, and *bankruptcy* of the parents. How would your informal trust be affected by these situations? And remember, with an informal trust, the children have access to all of the funds inside the trust upon reaching age 18. Are you comfortable with that? So what can be done?

All of the above concerns relating to informal trusts can be averted by putting the trust arrangement in writing and creating a *formal trust*. Consider getting the assistance of a lawyer or accountant with trust experience to establish a formal trust, to explain the pros and cons of a formal trust, and to outline the fees for establishing and maintaining a formal trust. In the end, you may see the decision of whether to create a formal trust as a cost/risk analysis. If the trust arrangement may have significant value down the road, there may be a greater desire to use a formal trust.

▼

Example

Herb and Sara just had a baby and have decided they want to start an education fund for little Zack. Together they visited their local financial institution and asked about setting up an in-trust account for Zack. The customer service representative explained that the institution offered such an account, and proceeded to tell Herb and Sara the important characteristics of the account: the need for one parent to be the contributor and the other the trustee of the trust account; the fact that Zack would have access to the money at age 18; and the desirability of investing the proceeds in an investment producing capital gains in order to shift taxation of the capital gains to Zack (likely resulting in no taxation if Zack has no other income).

Herb and Sara, after talking to their tax advisor, and understanding the details and risk of this type of account, completed an informal trust document prepared by the institution. They also agreed to purchase the institution's *blue-chip equity mutual fund* with the contributor's investment proceeds. They decided that Sara would contribute toward the account and Herb would be responsible for management. At this point they didn't know if they should consider a formal trust, but decided to revisit the issue in a few years, when they hope to have a better idea of how much money they will save for Zack. A formal trust seemed to make sense only for a more significant amount of money than they had invested right now.

STRATEGY #34

Use RESPs to Save for Your Children's Education

The cost of post-secondary education in Canada is rising every year. The rapid increase is leaving many parents with significant concerns about how they going to pay for university or college costs once their children graduate from high school. Some parents have started their planning early and have set up informal education "in-trust" accounts for their children, and they should be commended for doing so. But these parents, along with those who have no yet commenced a savings program, should not overlook the government assistance available in *Registered Education Savings Plans* (RESPs).

RESPs are tax-deferred savings plans intended to provide financial assistance with the cost of post-secondary education of named beneficiaries, typically children or grandchildren of a contributor. Although there is no *tax deduction* for the contributions (as with *RRSPs*), the earnings in the plan are not taxed until they are paid out to the beneficiaries as education assistance payments. And it is the beneficiaries who must include the accrued earnings in their income so there may be no tax at all if they have little other income.

The maximum amount that can be contributed annually for a single *beneficiary* is $4,000, with a lifetime maximum of $42,000. Contributions can be made for up to 21 years, and the plan must be collapsed within 25 years of its starting date. The federal government provides further assistance to those who use these plans, in the form of direct grants payable to RESPs under the new Canada Education Savings Grant program (CESG). The amount of the grant is equal to 20% of the first $2,000 of annual RESP contribution per beneficiary, or $400. And even if you don't make RESP contributions in a year, you earn entitlement to the grant ($400 annually), which will be paid to the RESP in the years that the RESP contribution exceeds $2,000 (20% of the excess, up to an additional $400). These grants are available beginning in 1998 for beneficiaries under age 18 and, therefore, the maximum lifetime grant for any single beneficiary will be $7,200. The grants will be included in the income of the beneficiary when they are paid out as part of the education assistance payments.

RESPs come in two broad forms: pooled plans and self-administered plans. Pooled plans are pre-existing plans with a number of subscribers, each naming particular beneficiaries. The annual contributions are generally preset and the plan investments are selected by the plan administrator. Self-administered, or individual, plans are set up by the contributor through a financial institution, *mutual fund* company, or investment *broker*. Contributions can be made in the amounts that you choose (up to the statutory limits) and you can participate in the investment decisions. More than one beneficiary can be named in an individual plan, often referred to as a family plan, but in this case, all beneficiaries must be related to you by direct lineal relationship or adoption.

What are the benefits of using a RESP over an *informal "in-trust" account* to save for education?

- RESPs offer an annual grant per beneficiary of $400.
- Income in the RESP is not subject to *attribution rules*. Any income (*interest* and *dividends*) earned in an "in-trust" account for a minor is taxed in the contributor parent's hands, so parents using these accounts often limit the investments to growth equities. Parents using RESPs are free to select any investment.
- RESP funds can be used only to fund post-secondary education costs (this includes tuition, books, equipment, accommodation, or any other cost relating to schooling), whereas "in-trust" funds belong to the child completely once he or she turns age 18 and can be used for any purpose at that time. Are you confident that your child will be responsible enough at age 18 to spend wisely the money you saved?

And what's the downside?

- Although the income can be returned to you if your child does not pursue higher education (and, let's face it, when you start one of these plans for a child aged two, you have no idea), it is taxable in your hands. But up to $50,000 (beginning in 1999) can be transferred to your RRSP if you have sufficient contribution room. Any excess over the amount that can be transferred to your RRSP will be subject to an additional penalty of 20%. The grant must be repaid.
- The amount you can contribute is limited and, at the rate that post-secondary education costs are increasing, there may not be enough money in the RESP to fully fund post-secondary costs.

The downsides can be mitigated in a number of ways. First, use a family plan for your children, so that only one of the children has to pursue higher education to benefit from the plan. If you are concerned that you will not be able to save enough using RESPs or you would like to set aside funds for your children for purposes other than education, you can certainly use "in-trust" accounts or *formal trusts* in conjunction with RESPs.

▼

Example

Francesca and Leo set up "in-trust" accounts for their three daughters, Lucy, Joanna, and Amanda, when the girls were born. The girls are now 2, 4, and 7 years of age respectively. Leo has been seeing a lot of press on the Canada Education Savings Grant program and he's beginning to think that perhaps he should have set up RESPs for the children instead of in-trust accounts. He had decided to go the "in-trust" route initially because he thought RESPs were too restrictive, he would be able to set aside more money for the children using "in-trust" accounts, and, because the children were so young, he had no idea whether or not they would go to university or college.

After speaking to an advisor, Leo and Francesca came to realize that RESPs have become far more flexible over the last few years. They could set up a family plan with a *discount broker* for a small annual fee and, if they contributed at least $2,000 per child annually, an additional $1,200 of grant would be paid to the account annually up to the year each of the children turned 17. They could choose a wide variety of investments and, as long as one of the girls attended university or college, all the earning could be paid out to that one child without adverse tax consequences to them (although a portion of the grant would have to be repaid).

The advisor did some quick calculations and determined that if Leo were to carefully plan the contributions so that he

141

would contribute the lifetime maximum per child of $42,000, paying at least $2,000 for each year that the child was under age 18, the plan could accumulate approximately $77,000 for the eldest child, $96,000 for the middle child and $108,000 for the youngest child by the end of the year each of the children turned 17, assuming a modest 8% annual return.

After some careful consideration, Leo and Francesca determined there was little risk in using an RESP. They liked the idea that they were saving exclusively for education, and were confident that at least one of the children would pursue higher education.

They decided to keep the "in-trust" accounts, because they were uncertain about how high the costs of post-secondary education would go and they might want to have funds set aside for their children for other purposes at a later date. However, they planned to fund the RESP first, and then put aside money "in trust."

STRATEGY #35

Hold Tax-Disadvantaged Investments Inside Your RRSP or RRIF

Tax-disadvantaged investments are investment products that generate highly taxed income such as *interest* income. *Tax-advantaged* investments are investment products that generate *dividends* or *capital gains* — income that is taxed at lower rates than interest.

While trying to keep your overall *portfolio* balanced, consider holding interest-bearing investments inside your *RRSP* or *RRIF,* and *stocks* and *equity mutual funds* outside your RRSP or RRIF. For individuals in the highest marginal tax bracket, this strategy can reduce, by up to 16%, the income taxes paid on investment income every year. (Interest is taxed at 50%, while Canadian dividends and capital gains are taxed at 34% and 38% respectively.)

If you currently hold interest-bearing investments outside your RRSP or RRIF and stocks or *equity* mutual funds inside your RRSP or RRIF, consider switching them. Assuming you are dealing with investments of equal value and won't be throwing your current balanced investment portfolio out of whack, tell your investment advisor to switch the *assets.*

143

Note this common mistake: many Canadians employ the above strategy and transfer *mutual funds* with significant accrued gains attached into their RRSP or RRIF. In that case, there is a *deemed disposition* on the investments on their transfer into the RRSP or RRIF. That means any *accrued capital gains* on the mutual funds moved into the RRSP or RRIF are realized and taxed on the transfer. The prospect of triggering this tax may cause individuals to re-evaluate the transfer of certain investments into their RRSP or RRIF. Where possible, look to transfer assets without significant *accrued capital gains*, such as *GICs* or Canada Savings Bonds.

Some may argue that you should ignore the tax impact as described above because if you own an equity investment earning 15% annually and a GIC earning 5%, the overall tax deferral advantage from holding the equities inside the RRSP or RRIF is more significant due to the larger return; some may also argue that I have my strategy backwards. My strategy is admittedly tax focused, and, as I always state, tax should be only one factor to consider in the development of an investment portfolio. However, I would point out that my strategy is also risk focused, meaning that investors should consider holding their riskier investments (equities) outside their RRSP or RRIF, because the chances of earning 15% consistently may be low (and thus the tax factor becomes important again), and because there is the risk of loss with equities — and any losses realized outside an RRSP or RRIF can be applied against other capital gains to reduce tax. Inside your RRSP or RRIF an investment loss is just a loss of capital to you.

▼

Example

Jeff has $5,000 worth of *stripped bonds* outside his RRSP, invested for the long term (assume *fair market value* and cost are similar in this example, although this may not always be the case in reality). He also has a $20,000 RRSP consisting completely of equity mutual funds. With his investment advisor, Jeff completed an overall assessment of his appropriate *asset allocation mix* and determined that owning 80% equities was comfortable. The advisor suggested, however, that Jeff consider holding some of the fixed income component inside his RRSP, in order to benefit from the tax-advantaged nature of the equities. Jeff liked the idea of saving tax without changing his overall portfolio — instead, just reorganizing it! — and asked his investment advisor to switch $5,000 of equity funds in his RRSP with the $5,000 of stripped bonds.

This was a *tax-smart* move by Jeff for two reasons. First, future taxable investment income (primarily dividends and capital gains) arising from the equity mutual funds will be taxed at a lower rate than the stripped bond interest. Second, stripped bonds can be a poor investment outside an RRSP due to their structure. Stripped bonds provide their return only at maturity, but you must pay tax on the return annually. In other words, you have an annual tax expenditure, with no income inflows to pay the tax when due. This may leave you searching for ways to pay the tax bill.

One drawback of this strategy is that Jeff's stripped bonds are "deemed to be sold" prior to their transfer to the RRSP, and a capital gain may be realized that will attract tax on Jeff's tax return next year. There is no tax bill in this case, though, and Jeff decided to proceed anyway. A larger potential tax liability might have caused Jeff to consider using some GICs for the RRSP transfer instead.

▼

Bonus Tip

A few words of caution about this strategy: before switching assets inside and outside your RRSP or RRIF, ensure that the move is consistent with your investment strategy and asset allocation. Also, ensure that factors such as your short-term cash needs are considered. Equity mutual funds may not be a good investment outside your RRSP or RRIF when you have a short-term cash flow need.

STRATEGY #36

Increase Your RRSP Contribution Room

It is generally in everyone's best interest to pack as much into his or her *RRSP* as possible. Besides contributing as much as possible and as early as possible to your RRSP using your regular contribution room, consider using some other techniques to get money into your RRSP.

Retiring Allowance

An employee leaving an employer due to either retirement or forced early departure may receive a payment for lengthy service called a *retiring allowance*. If the employer agrees to pay a retiring allowance, some or all of the amount may be automatically transferred into the employee's RRSP, tax free, based on eligibility criteria according to the *Income Tax Act*. Employees leaving their employers for one reason or another should consider negotiating their final pay package to include a qualifying retiring allowance. Consult a tax advisor to ensure that any payment received meets the criteria for a retiring allowance that can be transferred to an RRSP.

Increasing RRSP Contribution Room

RRSP contribution room is based on *earned income* in the previous year. Earned income consists primarily of *employment income* and *self-employment income*. Individuals with the ability to control their annual pay (e.g., owners of incorporated businesses) should consider paying themselves enough salary to contribute the maximum to their RRSP each year. To make the maximum contribution of $13,500 in 1999, individuals should pay themselves or negotiate to receive earned income of at least $75,000 ($13,500/18%) in 1998.

▼

Example

Murray owns a successful small company in which he is an active owner/manager. The *corporation* earns about $400,000 a year before taxes. He recently hired a new tax accountant, who reviewed his company's books for tax-saving opportunities. The accountant noted that Murray and his wife (who also worked in the business) were in the habit of drawing only $50,000 in salary from the business each year. The accountant pointed out that Murray and his wife should consider raising their salaries to at least $75,000 a year in order to be able to contribute the maximum $13,500 each to their RRSPs annually. This strategy could have several advantages for Murray and his wife:

- They would be able to increase the size of their RRSPs much faster and have a more comfortable retirement; this is the key benefit.
- They would receive a larger tax deduction annually by taking advantage of the larger related contribution room and actually contributing more.
- A special low tax rate applies to the first $200,000 of business income of Canadian private companies. Income

in excess of this amount is taxed at regular corporate rates. If the income in excess of $200,000 is kept in the corporation and paid out to shareholders in the form of *dividends*, some double taxation results (on the income in the company and on the dividend to the individual shareholder). For this reason, advisors often recommend that owner/managers pay out sufficient salary from a corporation to reduce the business earnings to $200,000.

- If their small business needs more cash to operate, Murray and his wife could always lend the money back to the company.

Crunching the Numbers

At their current salary levels of $50,000 each, Murray and his wife can contribute only $9,000 each to their RRSPs annually. But at $75,000 salary levels, they could contribute the maximum $13,500 each year. Assuming there is no change in the maximum contribution amount, and their RRSPs grow at 8% annually compounded, combined additional contributions of $9,000 ([$13,500 – $9,000] x 2) per year would result in additional savings of $411,000 in 20 years.

▼

A Word of Caution

An important point to note about this strategy is that it is more effective when the business is earning more than $200,000 annually and income is taxed at a much higher tax rate in the company than it would be below the $200,000 level. At income levels under $200,000 inside the company, the success of this strategy is more dependent upon significant tax-sheltered growth within the owner/manager's RRSP.

Business owners should consult a professional tax advisor to integrate company and personal tax-planning objectives.

STRATEGY #37

Build Your Child's RRSP Contribution Room Before Age 18

Does your child (under age 18) have a paper route? Does your teenager work in retail? If they do, you probably don't file tax returns for them, because their total incomes are too low to attract any taxation. Why bother, right?

While you may enjoy the fact that they don't pay taxes on their income, you may not be aware that their *employment income* qualifies as *earned income* for purposes of determining *RRSP* contribution room. A child earning $1,000 a year in salary may also earn $180 of RRSP contribution room (18% of qualifying income annually). While that may not sound like a lot of money, remember that the child will likely not withdraw the funds from his or her RRSP for another 55 years. The power of compounding, assuming (say) an 8% rate of return annually, will turn that single $180 of contribution into $12,000 in 55 years.

Better still, the contribution to the RRSP can be made by you, the parent, and the money can be invested on behalf of the child inside his or her RRSP. Moreover, the related *tax deduction* does not have to be claimed by the child immediately and can be accumulated and claimed in the future when the child's income is significantly higher and he or she can get more benefit from the tax deduction.

This strategy permits the accumulation of valuable RRSP contribution room early in life, and can start the power of compounding investment income potentially 15 years earlier than your children might otherwise start contributing on their own.

▼

Example

Jane has a son, Tom, who is now in university. Since Tom was 12, he has worked at part-time jobs in the summer to provide himself with spending money. Each year Tom earned about $1,500, except last year, when he earned $8,000 before starting university. Tom's income is low enough that he hasn't had to pay any income taxes. However, five years ago his mother starting filing tax returns for him anyway, in order to start accumulating his RRSP contribution room.

Last year, when Tom turned 18, Jane contributed $1,980 to his RRSP to get him started on saving for the future. Like many young kids, Tom didn't have the cash to make a contribution himself. By starting Tom's RRSP at age 18 instead of something more common like age 28, Jane ensured that the $1,980 deposited at that time and earning 8% compounded annually will grow to $108,000 by the time Tom is 69, compared to only $50,000 if the RRSP had been started at age 28.

▼

Bonus Tip

If you think this is a great strategy but have not been filing tax returns for your children for the past few years when you could have been, take note: you may be able to go back and file for the last three years. Filing tax returns for your children for the last three years will permit you to establish their earned income for RRSP purposes and build their RRSP contribution room. Consult a tax advisor about filing or amending previous tax returns.

STRATEGY #38

Invest in an RRSP Before You Invest in a Home

Here's your chance to go against the crowd: invest in a home at age 30 and an *RRSP* at age 20.

This strategy is the reverse of what many people do. People in their 20s typically get a job, get married, maybe buy a home, and have kids. They commit to a 15- to 25-year home *mortgage* which absorbs a lot of their cash flows during that period. During those 15 or more years, RRSP contributions may be made but are generally not maximized because it's hard to find all the necessary cash when there are so many other bills to pay.

Before they know it, people are in their 40s and the mortgage is nearly gone. It's finally time to turn their efforts toward their RRSPs, since retirement may be less than 20 years away. People may also realize at this time that they likely need at least $2 million in capital to live the retirement lifestyle they want, but have only 20 years left to accumulate this amount. In the end, they may not have $2 million when they retire, but they'll have a big, paid-off house!

Suppose instead that an individual in his 20s gets a job,

rents inexpensively or lives at home, and maximizes his RRSP contributions throughout his 20s, before getting married, having kids, and buying a home. In that period of time, the individual can build an RRSP with more than $50,000 in it, depending on his income, spending habits, and other factors.

Then, at age 30, he can purchase a home, and it too may be paid off in 15 to 25 years, although the payments will extend a little later in life due to the late start. Even if his RRSP contributions stop for 15 years, the value of the existing plan may grow to more than $200,000 in that period because of the tax-free compounding. When the individual is in his mid-40s, the mortgage is paid off and he can now continue to build on an already sizable RRSP.

The lesson to be learned here is that the power of compounding money is king. The longer your RRSP is in existence, the larger it will become with little effort or additional money from you. Given this fact, why not start your RRSP as early in life as possible? In addition to letting you build a larger RRSP, buying a home later in life will give you time to build up a larger initial down payment, and your earnings will likely be higher, permitting you to afford larger mortgage payments and reduce your mortgage faster.

One final word about real estate: this strategy assumes that real estate prices rise slowly. This strategy may not be the preferred route when it's possible to buy a home and take advantage of a rapidly rising real estate market.

▼

Example

Robert graduated from university at age 22 and took a job as a programmer with a growing computer company. The job paid $40,000 yearly and Robert immediately opened an RRSP and started making annual contributions of $7,000.

The investments grew at an 8% rate each year. By the time Robert got married to Deborah at age 29, he had $58,000 inside his RRSP.

Robert and Deborah bought a home that same year and selected a 15-year mortgage amortization period. They had managed to put down 10% toward the purchase. They also planned to apply any future income tax refunds as additional lump-sum payments toward the mortgage in order to pay it down faster. For the next 18 years, Robert and Deborah focused on meeting the costs of raising a family. Robert continued to make RRSP contributions, but they averaged only $4,000 a year during that time.

Now, at age 47, Robert has almost finished paying off his mortgage and is maximizing his RRSP contributions easily because of his larger salary and low debt. Based on his contributions and a growth rate of 8%, Robert's RRSP is currently worth $370,000 — even after his relatively small contributions over the last 18 years!

Robert was visiting his neighbour Emil last week. Emil is Robert's age, and the two have always compared their personal finances. Emil was quick to brag that he and his wife had paid off their home five years ago already and had no debt. They had a lot more money to spend on vacations, on the kids, and for investing purposes.

Robert listened quietly and then asked Emil about RRSPs. Had he been able to maximize his contributions, and how much had they been able to save? "We spent most of our spare money on the mortgage in our early years together," Emil said. "Then the kids came, so we didn't really start building our RRSPs until our mid-30s. Today our plans total about $200,000."

Robert smiled. He knew that his mortgage would also be paid off shortly but the early start on his RRSPs has resulted in a plan almost double the size of his neighbour's.

STRATEGY #39

Expand RRSP/RRIF Foreign Content Beyond 20 Percent

Inside your *RRSP* or *RRIF*, only 20% of the total cost of your investments can be in investments outside Canada. With more than 90% of the world's economic activity and investment opportunities occurring outside Canada, one might say that investing 80% of your life savings in a single, small corner of the world is risky. A widely diversified investment mix is an effective way to manage the risk of loss in your RRSP or RRIF *portfolio*. Owning investments in many countries is a form of *diversification*, which can reduce the adverse impact on your portfolio return if one of those countries has a bad year.

One way to invest beyond the 20% limit in your RRSP or RRIF is to purchase *synthetic index mutual funds*. A synthetic index *fund* replaces actual *stock* ownership inside an *index* fund with ownership of *futures* contracts that lock in the future change in a particular index. The *fund manager* invests much of the fund's money in Canadian *money market instruments* and uses the rest of the money to buy futures contracts on investments in foreign equity market indices like the S&P

500 in the United States or the Nikkei index in Japan. Futures are *derivatives*, and permit *money managers* to invest in the rise of an index without actually buying the stocks of an index. Because the cost of futures contracts is just a fraction of the cost of the underlying securities, synthetic index fund managers can buy large amounts of futures representing international investment exposure potentially far in excess of the permitted 20%.

Synthetic index funds should mirror the performance of the stock market indices they are designed to replicate. Stock market indices can represent the combined market value of many of the largest companies in a country, so, as an investor purchasing a country's leading index, you may be able to diversify across an entire economy without the risks and additional costs of picking specific companies to invest in.

To learn about investing in index funds outside an RRSP or RRIF, refer to Strategy #6.

▼

Example

Denise was reviewing her RRSP and was concerned about the large amount of Canadian content inside her plan. While the recent performance of the RRSP investments has been good, she felt uncomfortable that so much of her money was invested in one small country — Canada. Denise called her investment advisor, Diego, to see if there was anything she could do.

Over lunch, Diego educated Denise about the options available to increase the foreign content in her RRSP. Diego pointed out the following strategies:

• The 20% foreign cost limit inside her RRSP is based on original cost, but an increase in the market value of the foreign content will provide additional foreign exposure while cost remains within the 20% rule.

- In Canadian *equity mutual funds*, many of the *corporations* invested in by the funds are large multinational corporations. Since these corporations operate worldwide, their business is diversified and less susceptible to economic downturns in any one country. In effect, the investor is also invested globally, by owning these companies through the *mutual fund*.

- A Canadian mutual fund that is considered to be 100% Canadian for purposes of the foreign content rules may invest 20% of its holdings in non-Canadian investments. This means that Denise's 80% Canadian content may also have 20% foreign content. Thus, in total, she may have 20% foreign mutual funds plus another 16% (80% x 20%) foreign content inside her Canadian funds, for a total of 36% foreign content.

Diego summarized by noting that a regular Canadian fund may provide good exposure to non-Canadian investments but this may not be apparent without exploring the composition of the fund. A financial advisor can assist with this.

For additional exposure, Denise could consider purchasing *index mutual funds* that buy futures representing indices of other countries. Diego cautioned that whenever individuals invest outside Canada, they may also face gains or losses on currency from a rise or drop in the value of the Canadian dollar against the foreign currency they are investing in. This means that a gain earned from the rise of the Nikkei Index in Japan may be completely offset by a loss in currency value against the Japanese yen. Overall, because of currency fluctuations they may have no gain at all! Fluctuations in currency values arise from the impact of a variety of economic and political factors around the world.

Diego further explained that Denise shouldn't fear foreign currency fluctuations but instead should view investing in other countries and dealing with the ups and downs of currency as yet another form of investment diversification. More diversification can be good to further reduce risk of significant losses occurring in her overall portfolio.

Crunching the Numbers

Denise's Current RRSP Content:

LMN Cdn. Equity Fund	$4,000	100% RRSP eligible
RST Cdn. Bond Fund	$4,000	100% RRSP eligible
PQR International Equity Fund	$2,000	eligible as foreign content
Total portfolio	**$10,000**	
Investment outside Canada:		**20%**

Denise's possible RRSP content using synthetic funds (assuming she sold her current Cdn. equity fund and replaced it with a synthetic fund):

IND U.S. Synthetic Index Fund	$3,000	100% RRSP eligible
RST Cdn. Bond Fund	$5,000	100% RRSP eligible
PQR International Equity Fund	$2,000	eligible as foreign content
Total portfolio	**$10,000**	
Investment outside Canada:		**50%**

STRATEGY #40

Guarantee Your Investments with Life Insurance Seg Mutual Funds

The hot investment topic lately is *life insurance* segregated funds. These are *mutual funds* offered through life insurance companies in the form of an insurance contract, offering additional benefits compared to regular mutual funds. Many advisors are currently comparing the strengths of these life insurance products against "plain-vanilla" mutual funds.

Here is a summary of the advantages of these new seg mutual funds.

- Up to 100% of your capital is guaranteed at death (regardless of the period of ownership) and up to 100% of your capital (less withdrawals) is guaranteed after ten years (varies among insurance companies). These guarantees stand regardless of the fund's *performance* over this time period. Regular mutual funds offer no such guarantees, leaving you exposed to a loss on your original investment at any time due to *stock* market volatility.
- If your seg mutual funds increase in value, you can reset the guarantees (subject to certain restrictions) to take

advantage of the rise, lock in the gain, and re-start the guarantee at the new higher value.

- In certain circumstances, the fact that these funds are offered through life insurance companies offers protection against creditors in case of bankruptcy. With regular mutual funds, creditors could have a direct claim on these investments if you went *bankrupt*.

- With life insurance seg mutual funds, if a *beneficiary* is named for the fund, your *estate* can avoid paying *probate fees*.

Compared to regular mutual funds, there are many beneficial characteristics associated with these life insurance seg funds that would benefit the right investor. But every good product usually has weaknesses. Let's examine some of these concerns.

- While seg life insurance products have been around quite a while, seg mutual funds have "caught fire" only recently — and, no doubt, caught the eye of regulators and lawmakers as well. With such a short track record as a "mainstream" investment linked to mutual fund companies, one may argue that they have not been around long enough to test whether their guarantees, creditor protection, and probate-avoidance activities will stand both the test of time and government regulatory changes.

- Looking a little closer at their advantages, it is worth noting that, for the guarantees provided, many of the providers offering these seg funds are charging up to 1% on top of already high *MER* fees inside the seg mutual funds. Are the guarantees worth the high fees to the long-term investor? If you look back in time, you may be hard pressed to find a ten-year period in which an investor lost money in the *blue-chip equity* markets — so in the past at least, the value of the guarantee was questionable, yet you are paying up to 1% a year for it!

161

With the creditor-proofing protection that can be available, the effectiveness of this protection will depend on your personal situation. The protection against creditors likely won't apply if you buy one of these funds with your money the day before you go bankrupt. And for most Canadians, who have a low probability of ever going personally bankrupt, this feature is probably not necessary.

As for probate fees, the provincial governments can always change the legal and tax rules to include life insurance seg mutual funds for probate purposes. Further, probate fees in Canada can amount to 1.5% or more of an estate (actual fees vary by province) on the death of the individual. While seg mutual funds may be excluded from the estate assets subject to the probate fee, keep in mind that you will be paying up to an additional 1% or so in MER costs on these seg funds *every year* to avoid a 1.5% probate fee paid once on death. Does that make financial sense?

Another potential disadvantage of life insurance seg mutual funds is their treatment of *distributions*. As a life insurance product, the distributions of *interest, dividends,* and *capital gains* earned inside the funds are kept inside the funds until maturity. A senior who may require monthly income from this investment would have to consider selling a bit of the seg fund each month to generate this income. While this is not a significant disadvantage, it is worth noting that the guarantees of principal don't apply to these monthly withdrawals. The guarantees apply only to the investment that is never touched for the ten-year period.

Are These Funds More Tax Smart than Regular Funds (When Purchased Outside RRSPs or RRIFs)?

The quick answer is no. Income and gains earned inside the funds are not actually distributed to *unit holders*. Rather, these distributions are notionally allocated to unit holders for tax purposes.

This means unit holders may have to pay tax on distributions earned, and they will have to come up with the cash from somewhere else to pay the tax bill, since the distributions are kept inside the fund until the seg fund is eventually sold. On the bright side, the taxed distributions will become part of the cost base of the seg fund investment overall, reducing the future capital gain that may exist on the eventual sale of the overall fund investment. This tax treatment differs from regular mutual funds, where distributions may be physically distributed to you on a regular basis, and are available for your ongoing cash-flow needs.

It is also important to note that the ability to reset the guarantee on the funds after a period of rising value is not a taxable transaction.

So, Are Seg Mutual Funds For You?

Life insurance seg funds have some tremendous advantages compared to mutual funds but, as with most products, they will be more suitable for some than others. The guarantee against loss may be desirable for older investors who can't afford to lose money, those who are investing in the *equity* markets for the first time, and those people who have a low *risk tolerance*. The guaranteed return of some/all principal is a great way to provide these investors with peace of mind about their original investment, yet give them the upside potential associated with stock market returns.

The creditor-proofing feature, if set up correctly, can be useful to business owners, and professionals like accountants

163

and lawyers who operate through partnerships with no other protection of their personal wealth from legal challenges. And, for investors who want to borrow money to invest (*leverage*), seg funds can play a greater role than other investments in assisting you to create a leverage strategy.

But if you consider yourself a regular long-term investor, and don't fit into one of the categories above, you may be better suited with plain-vanilla mutual funds, and put the extra cost of seg funds back in your pocket every single year.

▼

Example

Helen is a 66-year-old widow. Although her health is reasonable for her age, Helen is concerned that her finances after her death will be taken care of. So she is always asking questions, and still stays involved in what is going on in the investment world.

Helen lives completely on her employer's pension, and really needs no additional *investment income* to live on. She tends to give her investment income to her children and grandchildren as gifts each year. Her investments amount to a small *RRIF* and $300,000 invested in *GICs*.

Donna, Helen's financial advisor, had recently discussed life insurance segregated mutual funds with Helen, and Helen was very interested. Today, Helen called Donna to reconfirm the features of the product, and then to consider a purchase.

Donna was pleased to hear from Helen and, after being prompted, she reviewed the features of these products that were suitable for Helen.

• The principal of the investment is 100% guaranteed (excluding withdrawals), meaning you will never lose your initial investment. Further, if you make money on the investment, you can add this to the guaranteed principal portion as it is earned.

• The potential returns are linked to the stock market, providing the opportunity to earn significant returns without the risk of losing your principal.

Donna's one word of caution concerned *liquidity*. If Helen needs annual investment income from this amount, these products may not be suitable because income would have to be generated from withdrawals from the funds. These withdrawals would not be subject to the guarantee of principal. Further, Helen will need to pay the taxes on the income and gains earned by these seg funds using income from another source (her pension), since all income earned inside the funds is kept inside the funds. To address this, Helen could consider investing only a portion of her taxable money in seg funds, an amount she will not need during her life.

Helen liked what she heard and is prepared to buy some of these seg funds. She asked Donna to set up an appointment for the next step — the process of reviewing all the seg funds out there to determine which specific products are best suited for her.

Donna agreed, and said she would be in touch once the meeting was booked.

STRATEGY #41

Protect Your Cottage and Your Business Using Life Insurance

On death, your cottage, your business, and all other *assets* owned are deemed to be disposed of for *fair market value*. This means that if the properties were purchased long ago at low cost but have greatly increased in value, the tax bill on death could be significant. So how does the *estate* pay the tax bill due on the final tax return of the deceased individual?

A large tax bill to an estate with few liquid assets could mean that the cottage itself or the family business interest has to be sold to non-family members in order to come up with the cash to pay the tax bill. Very often, family members do not want to sell a cottage that has been in the family for 50 years, or a family business that was supposed to be the future livelihood for the grandchildren. But sadly, the sale of the cottage or business may be the only choice for an estate with few other cash resources to pay the deceased's final tax bill.

These are two situations where purchasing *life insurance* to offset the tax liability on death can make a lot of sense. The policy will pay a tax-free benefit on death that can be used to clear up a large final tax bill arising from a *deemed disposition* of a cottage or business interest.

If ownership of a cottage or business interest will likely be transferred to a surviving spouse on death, the insurance policy should pay out on the death of the second spouse. Because asset transfers between spouses occur at cost, there is no immediate tax on the death of the first spouse. This type of insurance policy is called *"joint and last to die."* The insurance premiums may also be lower in this case, since the payout will not occur until the death of the last survivor.

▼

Example

Iris and her husband, Frank, have owned their family cottage since before their children were born. They purchased the cottage for $20,000, and it is now worth $320,000. Their children are now over age 30. Iris and Frank are planning to leave the cottage to their heirs on their deaths.

Iris knows that on the death of the last surviving spouse, there will be a tax bill of approximately $120,000 to be paid out of their estate before the cottage can be passed on to their children. Iris has been pro-active in taking steps to keep the cottage in the family, but she is concerned about the taxes that may be due on their death.

The entire family has grown up at the cottage, and no one wants to see it sold. To prevent this, Iris wants to purchase a life insurance policy that will pay the tax bill on death with the tax-free proceeds from the insurance policy. Iris has decided that she and Frank can afford to pay into a life insurance policy over the next 10 years. This cost will affect their cash flow during this 10-year period, but not too badly, and she will achieve a long-term objective that is very important to her and the entire family.

To implement their goal, Iris and Frank have scheduled meetings with three insurance agents, who will each propose a recommended solution and cost. Iris is also going to ask her *financial planner* (who is qualified to consult on life insurance) to sit in on the meetings and provide an objective opinion of the agents' products. Iris has never fully understood the "lingo" of life insurance agents, and she thinks that having the financial planner along to help her ask the right questions and compare the presentations makes good sense.

STRATEGY #42

Consider Universal Life Insurance as an Investment

Some *life insurance* products are becoming increasingly attractive as investment options, in addition to playing an important role in risk management. This strategy focuses solely on this investment component, which can be beneficial in the right situation.

A *universal life insurance* policy is a form of permanent insurance where the insurance component and the savings element are separate and distinct, and the policy owners may have several investment options to consider for the savings piece of the policy, along with flexibility on the timing and amount of premium deposits. The investment options for the savings component can include fixed income instruments, *GICs*, and *equity*-associated investments. These equity-associated investments can include products tied to the *performance* of the *TSE 300*, the S&P 500 in the U.S., and other internationally recognized indices. Policy owners do not purchase investments in these indices or their holdings; rather, the life insurance company agrees to pay a comparable rate of return to the change in the *index* (or indices) in question. Policies may have several investment options which can be varied according to a client's wishes (within the same insurance company). Selection of the type(s) of investments for the savings component of the policy should be made after careful consideration of your *risk/return* preferences and balanced with your total investment *portfolio* mix.

A universal life insurance policy can provide tax sheltering of death benefits paid out on the policy holder's death, if the policy qualifies as an exempt policy under the *Income Tax Act*. These death benefits will include the accumulations from the savings component of the policy, which can grow tax free inside the policy over the life of the policy. The investment accumulation inside a universal life policy is usually added to the original death benefit amount. If, however, the accumulated savings inside the policy are ever "cashed in" during the life of the policy holder, a taxable transaction can result.

Aside from tax, if you name an individual *beneficiary* of the policy, the proceeds of the insurance on death pass outside your *estate* and eliminate the need to pay *probate fees* on the proceeds. There may also be creditor-proofing opportunities associated with owning universal life insurance that are not available with non–life insurance company products.

So what should you be concerned with? For tax reasons, you should try to avoid cashing in the policy before death. That aside, when you are investigating universal life policies, factors to evaluate include the following:

- The number of investment options for the savings component of the policy. Consider a policy with options in a variety of *asset* classes.
- The company's rules and any fees for switching between different investments as your needs and *risk tolerance* change over time.
- The quality of the life insurance company. Purchasing a

universal policy may be a 50-year commitment, and you want the insurance company to be there in 50 years.

- The life insurance company's administration expenses, mortality costs, and other expenses. These costs may affect the success of your investment component if they are factored into the costs of the policy. The treatment of these and other costs may vary by company.
- Accountability of the insurance company. Will it provide minimum credits to the investment funds you select to invest in? The size of credits can be affected by the variables described in the previous point.
- The basis on which the insurance company pays bonuses into the investment component.

In addition to pure insurance objectives, universal life insurance can play a role in your estate plan and investment plan. Given the variety of uses, the wide selection of products available, and the tax and investment complications, careful evaluation of options should be made before purchasing. Consider seeking a second opinion from an accountant or advisor who has expertise with insurance products and can provide independent advice. Have a clear objective in mind when buying, and most importantly, ensure that the policy is affordable to you. There is no sense in buying a policy that rewards death, while the cost of the *premiums* hurt your lifestyle today.

▼

Example

Laurel, a senior executive, is looking for opportunities to reduce and/or tax-shelter some of her income and investments. She is 48, earns $150,000 annually, and is married with 20-year-old twins. She has ample excess cash flow between

171

herself and her husband, Doug, who is a doctor. Recently, her financial advisor introduced her to universal life insurance. Laurel seems a good candidate for universal life insurance for investment purposes. She has excess cash flow and can afford the cost of the premiums over the next 20 years while she and her husband continue to work. Laurel and Doug are already maximizing their *RRSPs*, and universal life insurance seems like a good next step for tax sheltering of investment income. Laurel and Doug also want to leave their children a fixed amount when they die. Although Laurel and Doug have the capacity to provide their children with significant funds, they want to keep their RRSPs and their investments for themselves to spend in their retirement, and they are not going to worry about how much of these amounts will be left for the kids. Instead, they would like to purchase an insurance policy that will provide the desired amount for the children — pay for the policy now and be done with it.

Before making the purchase decision, Laurel and Doug listened to several presentations and reviewed several scenario charts provided by their financial advisor. The advisor also provided examples of products from different life insurance companies, the pros and cons of each, and the costs of each. Laurel and Doug found all this data a bit overwhelming, so they enlisted their accountant to help objectively analyze the data and the strategy in general. Their accountant was experienced with life insurance products. The financial advisor, the accountant, and Laurel and Doug together concluded that universal life insurance was affordable and appeared to be a good fit for Laurel and Doug's particular needs. They decided to buy two smaller policies from different institutions in order to split the risk of going with just one company.

Laurel and Doug have scheduled the next meeting with their financial advisor to decide on what investments to purchase in the savings component of the policy. The advisor will help them develop a fit with their overall investment portfolio, after careful consideration of their risk tolerance, their other investments, and their expectations.

STRATEGY #43

Measure Affordability of Life Insurance Before Buying

There is an opportunity to reduce taxes payable by your *estate* on death, by purchasing a *life insurance* policy that will pay out on your death so that the proceeds will offset the taxes due by your estate. Such a policy can be funded with regular payments while you are alive. While this can be an effective strategy to reduce the impact of taxes on death, there are issues that need to be addressed prior to a purchase of life insurance for this purpose.

- Can you afford the purchase of life insurance? If insurance premiums will significantly affect your cash flow while you are alive, and adversely affect your standard of living, is it sensible? Why buy life insurance and sacrifice your current lifestyle to enhance your heir's lifestyle after you have died? Senior citizens who are barely making ends meet on a fixed income should not be convinced that they need to pay *premiums* to purchase insurance just "so the kids will get a larger estate." These seniors may be sacrificing their own lifestyles by forcing themselves to live on less in order to afford the insurance premiums. And the kids may not need — or want — a larger estate. The kids would usually rather see you take the extra cash you have while you're alive and spend it on a vacation to come and visit them rather than applying it toward life insurance you may not be able to afford.

Purchasing life insurance to offset taxes on death can be an effective strategy in the appropriate situations. Evaluate your estate goals and the affordability of these goals prior to purchasing a policy. And seek a second opinion from a qualified advisor who is not selling you the policy and has no vested interest in making a sale to you.

Group Life Insurance

Many employees may have some amount of *group life insurance* offered through their employment. Similar insurance may also be offered by professional bodies, associations, and other organizations with members or employees. Be cautious not to rely too heavily on this insurance to meet all your needs for insurance. In some cases, you may be better off not buying the employer's group insurance for one or more of the following reasons: 1) if you pay premiums, they may be higher than if you had purchased insurance on your own, since the premiums factor in employees of all ages and health types; 2) with an employer's group policy, you may have little or no control over the type and amount of the policy; 3) your employer may be able to cancel the insurance at any time; 4) if you leave the employer, some or all of the insurance coverage may be lost.

Employer-provided group life insurance can be appropriate in the right circumstances, but a close evaluation of the policy should be made in order to understand coverage, benefits, and restrictions. If you need life insurance, shop around and purchase a policy that contains policy enhancements you need. Utilize a professional insurance advisor who understands what is important to you when purchasing insurance and who can provide access to a large variety of product options.

▼

Example

Shirley and Joe are having a great retirement. They saved aggressively throughout their working years, and now are enjoying having the financial freedom to afford the retirement they desire. They haven't had to cut back on their spending in retirement, and they can afford annual vacations, golf memberships, and spending time with their grandchildren. That's why they were a little confused when their insurance agent approached them about buying life insurance — they didn't know why they would need any.

The agent explained that the very fact that they were doing so well was the reason for his visit. He stated that as their *RRSP* manager, he noticed that their RRSPs had done very well and now contained in excess of $2 million dollars. This money would continue to provide ample cash flow to permit Shirley and Joe to live their desired lifestyle. They agreed. They also admitted that they can't even spend all the income they receive and are just reinvesting it again. And they said they expect this to continue as they have no expensive future plans.

The agent explained that on the death of the last survivor, the remaining RRSP or RRIF would be fully taxable at that time and taxed at approximately 50%. Any accrued capital gains that exist on their non-RRSP or RRIF investments will also be taxed at that time. When you add to this the probate costs, legal and accounting fees to wind up an estate, and even funeral costs, a substantial liability results on death.

Taxes in particular can significantly reduce the size of an estate.

The agent suggested the purchase of a life insurance policy that would be funded by a series of payments. The policy would pay out on the death of the last survivor and would pay a tax-free benefit which could be used to cover the taxes and other expenses due on death.

The agent thinks that the policy is affordable for Shirley and Joe because they have excess cash flow to afford such a policy without affecting their lifestyle. It is also a good investment since the tax-free nature of the death benefit makes the insurance policy attractive as an investment. They may be hard pressed to invest the policy premium amounts and earn an equivalent rate of return in a taxable investment. Purchasing the policy may help to grow the value of their estate more than regular taxable investing. And having a large payout on death means that all the death taxes and other expenses on death could be offset by the insurance proceeds. This would leave a larger estate to the heirs.

Shirley and Joe agreed they had the surplus cash flow to afford such a life insurance policy. And the policy could always be cancelled if their finances worsened. They hadn't really thought before about maximizing their estate; they were prepared to give their kids whatever remained. However, if they could afford the insurance and it would serve to make their children more wealthy, they would consider it.

STRATEGY #44

Consider Donating a
Life Insurance Policy to Charity

In mid-life some people come to realize that they are carrying *life insurance* that they may not need. The insurance policy may have been acquired when they were younger, to provide funding to pay off a *mortgage* or to provide for a surviving spouse and children. However, once the mortgage has been paid off and capital has been accumulated to comfortably support family members in the event of death, the policy is really no longer necessary for its original purpose. In such a situation, the insured might stop paying *premiums* and allow the policy to lapse, or, alternatively, he or she might consider gifting the policy to a charity. There are tax benefits associated with this charitable gift, but it must be structured properly to enjoy these benefits.

For example, if the insured/donor merely names the charity as the *beneficiary* of the policy, he or she will receive no tax benefit at all. The premiums paid will not be considered to be a charitable gift eligible for the donation credit because the donor has retained ownership of the policy. On the death of the insured, the insurance proceeds will pass directly to the charity by virtue of the beneficiary designation, and not as a result of a charitable gift made by the insured and, therefore, cannot be claimed as a charitable gift made on death.

In order to qualify for a donation credit for the gift of the policy and the payment of future premiums, the insured/donor must not only name the charity as the sole beneficiary of the policy, but also transfer ownership of the policy to the charity. In this case, an official receipt may be issued for the value of the policy, which is generally the cash-surrender value plus any *interest* and *dividends* left on deposit. If there is a gain on the policy, it will be included in the income of the insured. In addition, the premiums that continue to be paid by the donor will be considered to be charitable gifts made in the year they are paid, and eligible for the donation credit.

Another way to gift an existing life insurance policy that is no longer needed is to name the *estate* as the beneficiary of the policy and to make a specific bequest in your will to a registered charity. No donation credit will be available for the premiums paid in this case. However, the bequest (the proceeds of the insurance policy) will be deemed to be a charitable gift made in the year of death. This could be a substantial amount, and the amount claimed as a donation can be up to 100% of net income for the year of death; any donation amount remaining can be carried back to the year prior to death, and again claimed up to 100% of net income of that year. Although the insurance proceeds would be subject to provincial *probate fees* in this case because they form part of the estate, the large donation receipt could offset a potentially substantial tax liability in the year of death.

▼

Example

Merideth and Henry were packing to move to their new condo when they discovered an old insurance policy that Henry had purchased 20 years ago. Henry had purchased that policy when they had two young children and a substantial mortgage. The premiums were automatically drawn from their savings account each month and, after such a long period of time, they had simply forgotten about it.

The insurance policy was for $150,000 and the annual premiums were $720. They chuckled when they found the policy. They remembered those early years when they were struggling and raising their family. But now Henry and Merideth were very secure financially. Their mortgage was paid off and both their children had graduated from university, were now married, and were becoming quite successful in their own careers.

Henry suggested that they should just stop paying the premiums and allow the insurance to lapse. After all, if Henry were to die, Merideth would be able to manage well with the wealth they had accumulated. Merideth agreed, but thought they should discuss the issue with their accountant first, just to make sure it was the right thing to do.

Henry called Selina, the family accountant and financial advisor, the next day. She suggested he come in for a quick meeting and bring the policy with him. After looking through it, Selina agreed that the insurance policy was not necessary because of their strong financial position. But she also knew that Henry and Merideth had been very generous to a number of charities over the last five years. She told Henry that he could supplement his philanthropic activities by gifting the insurance policy to one of his favourite charities. Henry liked the idea, because he always felt good about making gifts to charitable organizations. He asked Selina how to go about making the gift.

She explained that there were two alternatives. Henry

could name the charity as the beneficiary and transfer ownership of the policy to the charity. In this case, the gift of the policy would not result in a donation for tax purposes because there was no cash surrender value. However, if he continued to pay the annual premiums, he would have an annual donation eligible for *tax credit* of $720. The other choice was to name the estate as the beneficiary and amend Henry's will to provide for a specific bequest of the insurance proceeds, $150,000, to his favourite charities. Selina told Henry that, in this case, he would have a $150,000 donation in the year of death, which could result in a tax saving of about $75,000 in that year. He would have to maintain the policy and continue to pay premiums, which would not be considered donations eligible for the credit. Also, the $150,000 would be subject to provincial probate fees.

Henry discussed the issue with Merideth and they decided that they would continue paying premiums, change the beneficiary of the policy to Henry's estate, and change his will to include a bequest of the insurance proceeds to his favourite charity. They were very pleased that by continuing to make a mere $720 payment annually, they could benefit a charity substantially in the future and, at the same time, get a substantial tax saving.

STRATEGY #45

Evaluate a Life Insurance Trust

An insurance _trust_ is simply a separate trust (separate from the estate created on death) that receives the proceeds from your _life insurance_ policy on your death. These proceeds are then distributed according to any terms you specify. The benefits of using an insurance trust are as follows:

- Because the _trustee_ is the named _beneficiary_ of the policy (as opposed to your _estate_), the insurance proceeds do not form part of your estate and are not subject to provincial _probate fees._
- The insurance proceeds are protected from creditors.
- There is more flexibility than simply naming a individual beneficiary in the life insurance policy. You can set out a plan for _distribution_ in your will; it can be to various individuals and over a period of time, and you can provide the trustee with discretion on how the amounts will be paid out. Part of the insurance proceeds can even be directed to pay taxes that may be due on your death.

The insurance trust does not actually become a legal trust until the insured dies and the insurance proceeds are paid to the trustee. As a result, the insurance trust becomes a testamentary trust on death and, as such, it can benefit from the lower graduated tax rates. (An *inter-vivos* trust, which is a trust set up during one's lifetime, is taxed at the top marginal personal tax rate.) Because the insurance trust is separate from the estate, which is also a testamentary trust, there is the advantage of more than one set of lower *marginal tax rates* on the income earned on your total estate.

▼

Example

Pauline and Elliot own a *joint-and-last-to-die* insurance policy, which names the estate of the second to die as the beneficiary of the insurance proceeds. Their wills specify the terms and timing of distribution of their estates to their children. They chose this type of policy because it was less expensive than having two separate policies, and because each of them could adequately support the family alone. The intention of the insurance was to create an estate for their surviving children after they were both gone. They were content that they had set things up appropriately.

Just last week, Pauline and Elliot met with their accountant/*financial planner,* Bradley. They meet with Bradley every year to go over their current financial position and make any necessary modifications to their overall investment and financial plan. One of the things they asked Bradley to look at specifically was the adequacy of their life insurance.

After doing some calculations, Bradley determined that the insurance was adequate, but they could increase the value of their estate for their children by simply setting up a trust for the insurance proceeds. Elliot wasn't too keen initially. He had heard that setting up a trust was a complicated matter; there were all sorts of legal and accounting costs and loads of paperwork to deal with.

Bradley explained that there was very little legal work required. Pauline and Elliot simply had to change the beneficiary of the insurance policy to the trustee of this separate estate, and they could use any terms they wanted for the distribution of the insurance proceeds. In fact, they could use the same terms that were specified in the will for their estate. He also explained that there were really no ongoing costs because the trust itself would not be created until the insurance proceeds were paid out. And because the trust would be a testamentary trust, subject to the same marginal tax rates that apply to individuals, some income splitting might be accomplished because another set of low marginal tax rates was available for income earned after death.

Best of all, because Elliot and Pauline live in a province with high probate fees ($15 per $1,000 for estate *assets* in excess of $50,000), using an insurance trust, which would not be subject to probate, could save them as much as $15,000 in probate fees for their $1,000,000.

After hearing all this information, Pauline and Elliot decided that it would be a good idea to hold their life insurance policy in an insurance trust.

STRATEGY #46

Claim Investment Expenses as Tax Deductions

As part of *tax-smart* investing, you may incur a variety of expenses along the way. It is easy to overlook several tax deductions associated with investing. Here is a list of investment expenses that you can deduct annually on your tax return. Deduct these fees in the year they are paid.

* Safety deposit box charges
* Safe custody expenses
* Accounting expenses for record-keeping of your investments
* Investment management expenses
* Investment counselling expenses

Not all investment management and counselling fees are tax deductible; for example, fees to consult on an *RRSP* or *RRIF portfolio* are not tax deductible. Consult a tax professional to determine which of your fees qualify.

Here are a few more things to note about fees:

- Generally, in order to be tax deductible, fees must be incurred to earn income. This means that the fees being paid are undertaken to result in an income stream. Fees incurred with respect to your RRSP or RRIF are specifically not tax deductible.
- Many of us pay transaction charges and *loads* every time we buy or sell *stocks, bonds,* or *mutual funds.* Such fees are generally not tax deductible on your personal tax return. Instead, transaction charges for specific purchases are either added to the cost of the related investment or deducted from the proceeds of disposition.
- Today many investment institutions are giving clients the choice of paying an annual fee that is a percentage of the market value of *assets* invested, instead of the traditional *commission* charges according to the transaction you undertake.

From a tax point of view, the annual fee option is more attractive because you get an immediate *tax deduction* (assuming the fee doesn't apply to RRSP or RRIF assets, when it's not tax deductible) in the year incurred. With the traditional commission expenses, commissions are added to the cost base of the asset bought or sold. In this case, you will only benefit from the increased cost base from the fees when the asset is eventually sold. Further, the commissions will reduce the *taxable capital gain* — a gain that is taxed at a preferential rate compared to regular income.

The annual investment fee as a tax deduction will be applied against your total net income — meaning this deduction will reduce the higher-taxed regular income immediately. A tax-deductible investment expense is, therefore, worth more than a commission expense that will reduce a capital gain sometime in the future.

Note that the type of expenses you decide to incur, whether annual fees or commissions, should be based on an evaluation of far more than tax benefits and disadvantages. You should also examine frequency of transactions, among other variables, in concluding which route is best for you.

▼

Example

Every year Ted has his accountant prepare his tax return. This involves the tedious task of calculating Ted's gains and losses from his annual investment trading — a task that Ted's accountant does not enjoy. The accountant bills Ted $1,200 for this accounting work every year.

Ted's many trading activities are a result of his monthly discussions with a fee-based investment advisor. Each month Ted gets together with his advisor to discuss investment strategies and market conditions and to review Ted's portfolio. For each meeting Ted is billed $400, but he feels the regular meetings are helping him to invest better.

When Ted and his accountant got together recently to go over Ted's tax return, Ted complained about the high fees for the accounting and also mentioned the cost of his counselling fees. The accountant appreciated Ted's concern and pointed out that the cost should be evaluated on an after-tax basis. Both the investment bookkeeping fees and the counselling fees are tax deductible, meaning that at Ted's tax bracket — the highest (50%) — the extra fees are only costing him about half of what he pays upfront.

Ted was not used to thinking in "after-tax" terms, but agreed with the accountant that after-tax is what is really important. Learning that the fees were tax deductible helped him to understand the true cost of the services.

STRATEGY #47

Don't Get a Tax Refund

If your employer is deducting too much income tax from your pay cheque, it could be costing you a lot of money each year. Each spring, many Canadians look forward to receiving tax-refund cheques after filing their personal tax returns. A refund should be viewed with concern, however, not satisfaction. It means that your source deductions (the income tax withheld on your pay cheque) are all too high. It means that you are losing the benefit of having that extra pay in your pocket all year long; instead, you are loaning it to the government, *interest* free, until next April. This money, if invested in your name, could be generating income for you throughout the year.

You may be getting a refund because you claimed an *RRSP* deduction, or paid tax-deductible child care or alimony, or made a large charitable contribution. But your employer may not know you're contributing to an RRSP, or paying child care expenses or alimony, or making other selected payments that qualify for a significant deduction on your personal tax return. If your employer is in the dark, the source deductions from your pay cheque are being calculated assuming there are no significant deductions available. If too much income tax is being withheld, you have lost the opportunity to make money with the excess withholdings. Here's a way to improve the situation. Investigate whether your employer will send part of your salary directly to your RRSP by payroll deduction, eliminating the need for you to make the *RRSP contribution.* Companies that do this generally don't have to withhold income tax on the amounts so transferred.

Your other option is to mail in a request to the Source Deductions section at your local *Revenue Canada* Tax Services Office for a reduction in payroll withholdings. State what you earn. Include proof of your regular RRSP contribution or other qualifying significant annual deductions. Indicate that you expect these deductions to continue into the future. If your request is approved by the government, your employer will receive a letter from Revenue Canada authorizing a reduction in the amount of tax withheld. At this point you should start to notice the increase in your pay cheques!

▼

Example

Every April, Gwen would march around the office announcing how she would spend that year's whopping tax refund. She never thought much about the tax refund's origin — until she did some *tax-smart* planning.

Gwen realized that her annual refund was due to a combination of her RRSP deduction and her alimony tax deduction from the alimony she pays to her ex-husband. This year Gwen wrote to Revenue Canada explaining why she deserved a withholding-tax reduction: because both deductions should continue into the future, resulting in continued

189

refunds. She provided Revenue Canada with proof of her regular contributions to her RRSP and the future alimony payments she would make.

Revenue Canada agreed and told Gwen's employer to reduce her tax withholdings. Now she gets $55 more each pay cheque (after-tax) and has more cash in her pocket all year long.

Well, sort of. Gwen went one step further and increased her *mortgage* payments by the $55 extra cash. This $55 contribution against the mortgage principal each month allows Gwen to reduce the size of her mortgage faster.

STRATEGY #48

Make Your Interest Expense Tax Deductible

Borrowing as a Tax Strategy

Interest expense is generally tax deductible if the money is borrowed to earn income from a business or property. This excludes investments inside an *RRSP* or *RRIF*, but if you borrow money to purchase a *mutual fund* outside an RRSP or RRIF, the interest you pay on the loan will be tax deductible.

To make your interest expense tax deductible, complete the following process. Consider selling some of your existing investments to pay off any non-tax-deductible debt you currently have, and then borrow to reinvest. Be careful not to trigger any substantial *capital gains* on the sale of the investments. For example, you may have some Canada Savings Bonds or *GICs* and at the same time be carrying a *line of credit* balance or a vehicle loan. Use the investments to pay off the debts and then borrow again and purchase another investment outside your RRSP or RRIF. The interest on the newly borrowed funds becomes tax deductible since the borrowed funds are being used to earn investment income on the new investment. Note, however, that if you plan to sell investments with an accrued gain, you will be taxed immediately on any gain you realize. This is not a desirable result.

Don't try to shorten the process above by borrowing money to pay off the debts, leaving the existing investments in place, and then just saying that the new debt was incurred to invest. This will not be acceptable to Revenue Canada. To make the interest expense tax deductible, you should create a paper trail of documentation where you physically sell the existing investments, pay off the current debt, and then reinvest using the new loan proceeds.

Borrowing as an Investment Strategy

If your investment advisor is recommending that you borrow money to invest, and the advisor will earn greater *commissions* as a result, have him or her justify the reasons for the need to borrow. Take note that *leveraged* investments (investments purchased with borrowed funds) will have to earn a consistently higher rate of return than the loan in order to make the borrowing worthwhile. If you plan to borrow to invest, compare the after-tax investment rate of return against the after-tax cost of the interest on the debt. The after-tax investment return must exceed the after-tax interest cost in order for the strategy to be worthwhile. In other words, if the loan interest rate would be 10% for an individual paying 50% tax, then borrowing to invest would result in a 5% after-tax interest cost. This means that in order for leveraging to be worthwhile, the investment must earn greater than 5% *after-tax* each year the debt is outstanding.

If you borrow to purchase a fixed income investment or preferred shares, the related interest is deductible only up to the amount of income from the investment (for Canadian dividends, up to 1.25 times the dividend). *Common shares* have the potential to pay any amount of *dividends*, and therefore the interest should be fully deductible. In addition, capital gains are not considered to be income from property.

Therefore, if your investment has no potential to earn income, but only capital gains, the related interest is not deductible.

So the question is, will you be able to consistently earn a *pre-tax return* exceeding the pre-tax cost of the debt? Achieving a 5% after-tax rate of return year after year may be difficult to do. Using interest income and the same tax bracket, this would require a 10% pre-tax return each year. Futhermore, if you lose money on your investments purchased with borrowed money, the percentage loss is magnified significantly: you lose part of your original investment, still have to pay interest on a loan, and still have to repay the loan. Remember, you are offsetting a fixed liability with a variable *asset*!

So if you plan to borrow to invest, be cautious, as profitability is not guaranteed and the whole idea may not be as attractive as it first appears. As a long-term strategy, borrowing to invest can be a profitable undertaking. But when deciding whether to try this strategy, examine a few "what if" scenarios using different possible rates of return with the investments. And get a second opinion from a financial advisor who is qualified to determine if borrowing to invest makes sense for your personal finances.

▼

Example

Phyllis recently found herself incurring more and more interest expense on her monthly credit card bill. She just couldn't get ahead and wanted to do something about it before it got out of control. So Phyllis went to see her financial planner about her predicament. Her financial planner noticed that Phyllis had $5,000 in Canada Savings Bonds she had accumulated for no particular purpose. The planner suggested to Phyllis that she cash in the bonds and pay off her outstanding credit card bill completely. The planner also suggested that Phyllis get into the habit of paying off her credit card bill in full each month in order to avoid incurring high interest charges. The planner commented that if Phyllis didn't have the money to pay off the credit card, she should consider getting a lower-interest consumer loan from her financial institution and using the proceeds to pay off the credit card bill — in effect, replacing more expensive debt with less expensive debt to improve her cash flow.

Phyllis followed the financial planner's recommendations by cashing in the bonds and paying off the debt. Her credit card company was charging her interest at 15% annually. Since this interest was being paid with after-tax income, at her 50% *marginal tax rate* the interest expense was costing her 30% interest in before-tax dollars. Just by paying off this interest expense, she arguably earned an incremental rate of return equal to the difference between 30% and what she had been earning on the investments she sold to pay the debt.

The planner had also recommended that if Phyllis wanted to increase her ability to invest, she should consider borrowing from her financial institution and investing the proceeds in an investment that meets her needs and risk preference. This strategy would make her interest expense tax deductible since the loan proceeds would be used to buy investments that would generate investment income. But in this case, Phyllis decided not to borrow to invest. She didn't want more debt, and was more concerned about extinguishing her credit card debt.

▼

Bonus Tips

- Some credit card companies in Canada still charge you interest on the entire balance outstanding on your bill, *after* you make a partial payment. Only when you pay off the entire amount outstanding do the interest charges stop. So try to pay all of the balance due each month.

- Sometimes investors borrow money to invest, lose money on the investment, and are then left with a debt to pay and no investment. Upset with the loss, many investors will make it a priority to pay off this investment debt — but that may not be the *tax-smart* thing to do. Even with the related investment wiped out, the interest expense on the investment loan can continue to be tax deductible. It is wise for an investor to apply free cash flow to non-tax-deductible debt (e.g., a *mortgage*, credit cards) first, because that interest expense is not tax deductible.

- Beware Revenue Canada's superficial loss rules. These rules prevent a taxpayer or his or her spouse from claiming a loss for tax purposes after selling a losing investment to realize a loss and then repurchasing the same investment. When reinvesting, invest in different securities, or wait at least 30 days to reinvest in order to avoid the superficial loss rules.

STRATEGY #49

Reduce Capital Gains Using Capital Losses

When you invest in *stocks* and *equity mutual funds*, you hope to earn *capital gains*. Because the price you pay for the stocks or equity mutual funds can go up and down on the stock market, you may earn a capital gain or a *capital loss*. A capital gain or loss is the difference between your proceeds on sale and the original cost of the investment. A capital gain will be taxed at approximately 38% for a Canadian in the top marginal tax bracket.

Here are two strategies to help you minimize that tax. If you plan to sell the investment with the gain near the end of the year, consider waiting until after the final trade date that settles in the same year (there are three business days between trade and settlement date). The gain will then be taxable in the next year, and tax will be due in April of the year after that; a nice deferral of tax for a short period of time. Of course, the tax motive for this strategy becomes secondary if you need the funds from the sale immediately and can't afford to wait to sell, or if investment market conditions warrant an immediate sale.

A second strategy is to sell another stock or equity mutual fund that has an equal-sized capital loss, before the end of the year. For tax purposes, capital gains and capital losses offset one another when they occur in the same calendar year. It is worthwhile to review your *non-RRSP/RRIF* investment *portfolio* before the end of each year. You may have losing investments that it makes sense to sell to reduce your tax bill on the successful investments you sold during the year.

Keep in mind that you shouldn't sell investments with a current accrued loss just to reduce your tax bill. Sell investments you were planning to sell anyway, or sell investments that make sense to sell for the right investment reasons. And if you own investments that are currently in loss positions but you want to hold on to because you think they will rebound, you could still sell the investment, trigger the loss, and repurchase the same investments after 30 days have passed. Note that neither you nor your spouse can repurchase the investment within 30 days before or after the sale of the old investment or else you will be denied access to the capital loss.

▼

Example

Wayne likes to dabble in the stock market and has had a pretty good year so far. As of the end of November, he had capital gains of $14,000 that will be taxable for this year. But Wayne suddenly realized he had two problems. First, he had already reinvested the proceeds from these gains and didn't have the cash available to pay the taxes due on these gains next April. Second, he doesn't like to pay taxes. He was wondering what to do.

Wayne was talking to his neighbour about his investment successes and failures this year. The neighbour told Wayne to consider selling some of his investment "losers" to realize capital losses that would offset the capital gains. Only the net taxable capital gains for the year are taxable. If he could offset the gain completely, he wouldn't have to pay any tax on the gain next April.

Wayne liked this idea and went to his investment advisor to evaluate his investment portfolio. Together, Wayne and the investment advisor evaluated all of Wayne's investments. Some of his loser investments still had promise and the two decided it made sense not to sell them. There were other investments, however, that they believed had no hope of ever producing a gain. In the end, Wayne decided to sell a few investments before December 31, for total capital losses of $8,000.

The losses reduced the net gains for the current year to $6,000 and his taxable capital gain to $4,500. While Wayne still has to pay some tax, he finds this amount much easier to swallow. He realizes that overall he is still better off, since he made money realizing the gains in the first place!

STRATEGY #50

Beware Offshore Tax Havens

For most of us, the idea of placing money offshore, out of the hands of Revenue Canada, is a pleasant dream. In reality, there are few opportunities for the average Canadian to defer or eliminate tax using a legitimate *offshore trust* strategy.

Canadian residents are taxable on their worldwide income. This means that as long as you live in Canada, you are generally required to report all income earned anywhere in the world, regardless of how or where, on your Canadian tax return. This generally includes income in an *offshore trust* where Canadian residents have an interest in that trust. There are some exceptions, however, to this general rule in the context of offshore trusts. If the trust is established by a non-resident settlor — the contributor of the property in the trust — and has a non-resident trustee, the undistributed income will not be subject to Canadian tax if the settlor is a resident of Canada for less than 60 months. Income distributed to a Canadian *beneficiary* will be taxable. This exception is particularly useful in the context of the multi-national family where different family members are resident in different jurisdictions and there is a genuine intention by the non-residents to benefit the Canadian residents.

Without getting into a lot of detail, this is what to remember about offshore tax havens: if you are a conservative Canadian with average wealth, you plan to always live in Canada, and your relatives are Canadian and will likely always live in Canada, there are generally no opportunities to save tax on investments using a legitimate offshore strategy. However, if you are ever planning to leave Canada permanently, if you have relatives who are not Canadian and want to become Canadian, or if these non-Canadian relatives want to leave you family *assets* from their *estate*, then you should consider consulting a qualified tax advisor about offshore tax strategies.

For individuals in Canada who believe that placing money in an offshore bank account and not reporting income on your Canadian tax return is an acceptable offshore strategy, be warned that your strategy is against the law. Since you are taxed on your worldwide income as a Canadian resident, you are obliged to report all of your income. If you choose not to report any offshore income, you are committing tax evasion and may face fines and imprisonment for these actions.

Where it is possible, planning the use of offshore trusts should be very carefully structured and paperwork should be precisely prepared. Properly done, this is legitimate tax planning and is not a form of tax evasion. Due to the complexity of this type of planning, ensure that you deal with a global tax advisory service that can deal with the cross-border international issues.

▼

Example

Mitch was an executive and liked to be aggressive with his income taxes. He prepared his own tax return and was always looking for new ways to minimize income taxes paid to

Revenue Canada. He was always reading about opportunities to invest outside Canada to avoid Canadian tax, and he finally decided to try one.

Mitch applied to open an account with a financial institution in the country of NoTax. He saw the ad in a local newspaper, and while he had never heard of the company, he decided to proceed without any additional research. He filled out the application and sent off the cheque. That was three years ago. Since then, Mitch has never reported the income he has earned from the offshore investment, and he thinks he has created the ideal offshore *tax shelter*.

Mitch's best friend, Fred, is a tax accountant. Mitch and Fred are close, but up to now they have separated their social and business relationships, and Fred has never given Mitch any tax advice. With Revenue Canada's recent proposed changes requiring Canadians to report certain investments outside Canada (a law that never existed before), Fred thought he should point this out to Mitch.

Mitch appreciated the information, but stated that it didn't affect him. He said he had money invested far away, beyond the reach of Revenue Canada. Fred looked at Mitch with alarm and stated that wherever Mitch's money was, it might not be beyond the government's reach. Revenue Canada taxes Canadians on their worldwide income, and it is the duty of all Canadians to report all their worldwide income on their tax returns each year, or potentially face penalties if Revenue Canada ever finds out they aren't.

Mitch turned white. While he had enjoyed minimizing income taxes paid by investing outside Canada, he had always wanted to do it within the realm of Canadian law. He told Fred,his entire story, and asked what to do. Fred said that he would help, and that they should refile Mitch's tax returns for the last three years to reflect the unreported income. Mitch may have to pay penalties and interest on the late payment of taxes, but since Mitch will be voluntarily telling all, it may be possible to ask for the penalties to be waived (not the *interest* on the overdue taxes).

BONUS STRATEGY #1

Stop Chasing Returns: Have a Plan Before You Invest

When you invest, are you looking for the highest possible returns? Do you buy the top 10 current funds, hire the star who is flavour of the week, or place money in the hands of *money managers* who think they can time the market?

STOP!!! Would you buy an airline ticket before deciding on a destination? Would you shop for a dinner party before deciding on a menu and guests? Then why would you purchase investment products without an overall plan . . . a financial plan?

Investment products are merely a means to an end. Before investing, determine what your "end" is.

Before you invest another dime, take one big step back and figure out what you actually need in returns to accomplish your personal and financial goals. You might be pleasantly surprised to discover that you don't need those high returns to accomplish your goals, which means you don't have to assume as much risk.

The returns you need and should aim for will depend on a variety of factors, including your current savings, your day-to-day cash flows, anticipated large capital outlays (such as a cottage or a boat), education savings needs, retirement plans, *estate* wishes, current insurance levels, and your tax position, just to mention a few. Let's briefly examine some of these factors and see how they fit into the plan.

Cash flow review — We're not talking about a detailed examination of your spending or the deposits and withdrawals from your chequing account. This process involves a bird's-eye view of your annual cash flows to determine current spending and annual savings, and to project future cash flow requirements. A look at cash flows is critical, because they are affected by all other factors.

Retirement plans — No matter how far off retirement is, you likely have an idea of the type of retirement lifestyle you want. You'll have to make a number of assumptions in this step, including the number of years to retirement, where you plan to live, how much traveling you plan to do, and your expected health. Current living expenditures will likely be used to project your future regular cash requirements. You want to define your retirement plan to figure out what you need to get from your investment *portfolio* to make that plan a reality!

Insurance needs — Insurance is an integral part of your financial and estate plan. The types and the amount of insurance you currently own should be examined to determine if they are appropriate for your particular needs. You may discover that you are overinsured, in which case the cost of those extra *premiums* could be reallocated for other important needs.

Estate wishes — You may want to leave your heirs as much money as possible, but does it make sense to compromise your current lifestyle to enhance the lifestyle of your heirs after you have passed away? You may find that your children would be happier if you spent more of your money, perhaps to visit them more frequently.

Life insurance is often sold as a means to pay taxes due on death and to maximize an estate. Only if leaving a large estate is clearly one of your objectives, and the insurance premiums are affordable, should you purchase such insurance.

Small business integration — Because small businesses are so closely linked with their owners, a small business owner's personal financial plan would be incomplete without taking into account the income generated from the business, associated taxes, potential growth, potential business risks, and various other factors that would affect the cash flows and *net worth* of the owner.

Educational savings — It is imperative that parents plan for the soaring costs of post-secondary education in Canada. This means saving enough to fund these costs when they arise so you don't eat away at savings tagged for other goals.

Taxes — Because income tax is likely the largest regular cash expenditure an individual makes, *tax planning* — and that means tax minimization and tax deferral — deserves constant and significant attention from qualified and experienced tax professionals.

Taxes should be a consideration point in each and every element of a financial plan.

- Retirement plans should be completed to optimize after-tax flows.
- Life insurance has tax advantages and disadvantages.
- An effective estate plan attempts to minimize tax on death.

- Small business owners can implement a number of strategies that will reduce overall taxes paid by the family and the business.

- There are tax-effective means of saving for education, resulting in a greater build-up of education funds.

With taxes playing such a significant role in every aspect of your financial plan, don't scrimp on professional tax planning. And remember, income tax laws are constantly changing, so you must revisit tax planning at least once a year. And let's not forget the tax effects on investment returns. Many investment advisors in Canada are paid to maximize your total returns — the returns you see reported in the papers. But what you should really care about is the return in your pocket, after taxes have been paid. Your investment planning should be aimed at maximizing after-tax returns, not *pre-tax returns*. An investment sales person may not be the most appropriate person to build a tax-effective investment portfolio.

It's Finally Time to Invest!

Once you've addressed all the elements of your financial goals, you can begin to construct an investment portfolio to meet your needs. Now, instead of building a portfolio to get the best returns, you're building a portfolio that manages risk. It may sound boring, but why aim for the big wins in risky funds when all *you* need to earn, based on your defined plan, is perhaps a 6% annual return? You'll achieve your goals and at the same time have many more restful nights.

Break away from the pack that tends to chase the hot money manager with the big returns, and construct a disciplined portfolio that will generate what you need (across every personal finance area of your life) while minimizing risk along the way.

Example

Cindy and Jim were finding that the amount of time they were spending on their personal finances was cutting into their personal time, and the stress from making investment decisions was getting to them. They decided to interview two financial advisors to compare their approaches.

Skip, the first financial advisor, was fast-talking and professional. He chatted with Cindy and Jim about what they wanted to do with their lives financially, and quickly focused the discussion on how they would achieve their goals with *mutual funds*. Thirty minutes into the presentation he was showing them *performance* results from several mutual funds, describing how each fund would be appropriate for them. Cindy cut the meeting short after an hour, because the second advisor was about to arrive. Without having anyone to compare him with, Cindy and Jim thought Skip had satisfactorily discussed their financial needs.

Tess arrived shortly after Skip had left. Sitting down, Tess opened up with a biographical description of her education and experience, and left a short resumé with Cindy to read later. Tess also questioned Cindy and Jim about their financial goals and needs, but pushed into far more detail than Skip had. Here is a summary of her notes:

Cindy and Jim's cash flow: Currently $100,000 gross income; $65,000 disposable income, of which they are saving $18,000/year in *RRSPs*, and $3,000/year outside RRSPs. I have left them with a detailed budget questionnaire to fill out to collect all cash flow details.

Cindy and Jim's tax position: Expected to be approximately 50% bracket until retirement, at which time it will drop to 41%. I will verify this from their last year's tax return.

207

Cindy and Jim's insurance needs: They are currently paying $1,500/year for $2 million of term insurance. We will complete a more thorough evaluation of their life insurance and *disability insurance* needs. They have agreed to provide copies of their policies. They plan to own these policies only until their child is grown.

Cindy and Jim's retirement plans: Cindy and Jim want to live on the same amount of disposable income as they have in pre-retirement, rather than assume a decrease in their cost of living. We will complete some forecasts of future cash flows, making some assumptions, to see if they are on track to meet their retirement goals.

Cindy and Jim's estate plans: Cindy and Jim want to leave an estate of approximately $1 million to their one child. This amount should be after all estate taxes are paid.

Cindy and Jim's educational savings plans: Cindy and Jim expect to incur $15,000 educational costs for their child over a 5-year period starting 15 years from now. They have opened an *RESP* and are contributing $2,000/year.

Cindy and Jim's current investment portfolio: They have combined RRSPs of $280,000, and non-RRSP savings of $25,000. They are fortunate to own their home (worth $300,000) outright, thanks to an inheritance that went towards paying off their *mortgage*.

Overall Question: What annual compounded rate of return on their investment portfolio is needed in order to enable Cindy and Jim to reach all of their goals and dreams?

An hour had passed. Cindy and Jim felt they had told their life story to Tess, and Tess thanked them for being so complete with the information. She explained how important it is to examine all financial needs in creating an investment portfolio, because the portfolio has to generate results that help to achieve objectives across a variety of financial areas in your life. In other words, you can't examine investments on their own, nor can you start immediately looking at investment products. The planning aspect is far more important than the eventual product you buy, and the planning for financial needs must be integrated. Tess explained how she would help Cindy and Jim as their overall financial manager — the person who would see the big picture with them, while also dealing with all the details. Someone who would treat the investment products they buy as no more than a means to an end, rather than the starting point.

Tess would be the person who would answer the question of their necessary rate of return on their overall portfolio, the return that will unlock their dreams. The necessary rate of return is a minimum objective each year. Using their necessary rate of return and considering Cindy and Jim's cash flows, taxes, and objectives across all planning areas, Tess can help them build an investment portfolio to reach their goals.

BONUS
STRATEGY #2

Don't Invest Based on Performance Alone

You've all seen lists of top-performing funds in business magazines, newspapers, and books. So, you may think, all you have to do is pick Canada's hottest *mutual funds* and you will earn impressive returns, right?

It doesn't seem to work out that way. Investors buying top-performing mutual funds may not make much money, and may even lose money, as last year's winner becomes this year's underperformer. And because investors jump onto the fund bandwagon *after* a fund has already made a big upward move, and then jump off when returns slump, we see the classic investment mistake, "buy high, sell low," which we all know is a recipe for poor investment returns.

Yet it should not be surprising that choosing a current top performer may prove disappointing. Even magazines and newspapers that publish fund-return rankings acknowledge that past *performance* is no indication of future success. Too few people realize that, all else being equal, this year's top-performing fund is no more likely to achieve above-average results next year than a fund that had a mediocre return.

The reality is that research has proven that excellent performance by a fund has more to do with the cyclical nature of markets and how the investment strategies and styles of *money managers* react with current market conditions. Successful money managers will stick firmly with a selected management style (e.g., growth or value), and, as a result of natural business cycles, there will be times when the fund will outperform and times when it will underperform. Trying to guess which management style will be more effective at any given time will require a crystal ball.

What to Do
First and foremost, don't pick your investments by performance rankings alone. Performance *is* relevant, but *only in the context of factors that contribute to performance.* In other words, **don't buy funds, buy fund management teams.**

Here are a number of underlying factors that should be considered in building your investment solution:

- **Management style of the money manager.** Management style (e.g., growth versus value) is a leading factor in determining performance, and *diversification* by management style helps to minimize risk of significant loss as the economy changes. Build an investment *portfolio* that consists of money managers using different management styles that react differently to the market cycle and economic conditions. When one money manager is winning, the other may be losing, but overall your returns should be more stable (and less volatile) over the long term.
- **Historical performance of money managers within a style.** The only way to fairly evaluate money manager performance is to compare managers using the same management style — apples to apples, so to speak. This way you can compare the particular manager against peers who will all benefit (or suffer) from the same mar-

ket conditions. Comparing managers with the same management style lets you pick out the true overachievers.

- **Long-term records of money managers.** You really have to wait more than five years to evaluate a money manager's performance under varying market conditions. If, however, you want to invest with an up-and-coming money manager and you feel comfortable with the firm and its investment process, you might want to make a small purchase initially. But put the serious money with long-established money managers who have proven themselves over several market cycles. And, remember, because you are buying a money manager, not a fund, trace the manager's records back through any previously managed funds.

- **Risk as it relates to return.** One cannot focus on return without contemplating the associated risk taken to generate the returns. In other words, higher returns are usually associated with higher risk. A money manager who had stellar returns last year because of some big wins on penny mining stocks gives a much different comfort level than a money manager who generated great returns because he or she had broad ownership of Canadian banking stocks.

- **Fees — on their own, and in comparison to peers.** With such high investment returns the last few years, many people haven't given much thought to fees. And with many of the fees buried inside products and netted against returns, it can be difficult to find out your total costs. The reality is that there are wide discrepancies in the levels of fees charged, and comparison shopping is critical. Even more important is questioning the value of the advice you get for the fees you pay.

- **Qualitative characteristics that can determine a money manager's future performance.** In evaluating successful money managers, you want qualities that will permit the manager to continue to be successful. Here are some questions that can be used to evaluate the qualitative characteristics of a money manager.

Organization
- Is the organization structurally sound, with strong leadership and a long list of reputable clients (e.g., pension funds, charities, endowment funds, and other organizations that would have done extensive research on the quality of a money manager before hiring one)?
- Is the organization going through any type of management reorganizations or buyouts, or is it losing staff to competitors, etc.? Either of these would cause distractions within the organization that may affect the ability of money managers to concentrate on investing.
- Has the organization been gaining or losing major clients recently? Why?

Processes
- Does the organization have a sound investment philosophy and money management style, and is that philosophy applied consistently in its investment *portfolios?*
- Has the firm mastered its core competencies and stayed away from being everything to everyone?
- If the organization is growing rapidly, how is it dealing with the demands associated with the growth? Has its style remained consistent as *assets* have been added?

People
- Are the money managers who built the firm's track record still making the investment decisions, or are less-tenured managers at the helm? Has the succession of portfolio managers been planned?
- If one *star manager* left the organization or died, would the portfolio management be significantly affected? Do you want to put all your eggs with one hotshot who may not be around next year?

- Do the money managers own *stock* (*equity*) in the money management company to link them directly to company success (and reduce their desire to leave)? What has employee turnover been like, and why?

Remember, there is no magic in picking winners, and you need to consider far more than past performance. To implement effective investment solutions, you must first understand the factors that can lead to success. Then, with a disciplined selection approach, you can hopefully achieve results that are consistent with your objectives.

▼

Example

It's Thursday morning, and Qwan is reading the local newspaper's monthly report on mutual funds. Through his self-directed *RRSP*, Qwan uses this report to review performance of funds in order to decide what to buy next. Qwan's investing success has been strong over the last few years, and he is confident in his ability to pick winners.

The phone rings. It's Lori, a friend of Qwan's from the gym. Lori and Qwan often chat about investing, as Lori also does her own investment research and purchasing.

As Qwan explains that he is hunting for his next purchase, Lori asks what Qwan does to get comfortable with his next purchase. Qwan seems puzzled, and doesn't answer. He expects the past performance of the fund to continue in the future. Then Lori asks what makes him think the past performance will continue in the future?

Qwan has no answers. He never really thought about it before. He typically bought the *hot fund* of the month, with the hotshot *fund manager* advertised in the newspapers or on TV. While he has done well recently, he never thought about it more deeply than that. He asked Lori for an overview of some of the other things he should be examining.

Overall, according to Lori, the most important aspects to consider in buying an investment are qualitative, not quantitative, factors. The numbers represent the past — not the future. In order to assess whether the future will resemble the past, you need to examine factors that led to the past successes. Some of these factors are as follows:

* Who are the people actually picking the investments inside the fund? What are their professional qualifications and experience? Are they responsible for the past successes, or did they just arrive on the scene? Do they own part of the *fund company* and are, therefore, motivated to make it successful (and not to leave soon)?
* What investment management philosophies, style, and processes does the manager use? Does this structure complement your other investments?
* What are all the costs of this investment, and how do these costs compare to the costs of similar investments? Is any extra cost worth it?
* Is the money management organization a quality organization? Is it able to handle growth, present a focused business strategy, minimize employee turnover, and minimize client turnover? Why is it losing clients, if any? A sound organization is the core to future investment success.

Lori promised to email Qwan a list of other factors to consider when purchasing investments. Qwan thanked Lori and, for the first time, realized that past investment performance is nowhere near the most important factor to consider when purchasing investments.

BONUS STRATEGY #3

Life Insurance Needs for Your Entire Life: A Blueprint

When it comes to *life insurance*, it seems many people are in the dark. Term insurance, permanent, *universal life*, term to 100: it seems different agents support different types for similar situations, recommending products that provide no easy comparison.

At the very least, ensure that you comparison shop for insurance by asking at least two insurance agents to propose on your needs. Now beware — insurance agents will say they offer broad choice among insurance company products. But don't settle for this — what you are after is advice on the appropriate type of product for your needs, which may vary between advisors. So use at least two different agents.

The following is a guideline that fits many Canadians who work for a living and lead average lives. If you have special needs, own a small business, or have complex financial affairs, professional insurance advisors should be consulted to assess your life insurance needs.

Nearing Age 30

When I say you are under age 30, I mean that you have no dependents (e.g., children) and no *mortgage*. In this situation, if you were to die, there likely would be no financial burden to anyone and generally no need for life insurance proceeds. (Savings should be enough to cover your funeral expenses.) If this is the case, you likely don't need any life insurance at all.

Getting Married

If your spouse is earning an income and is not a dependent, and you don't own a home, once again you may not need any insurance. If either of you died, the other would be financially self sufficient. No doubt both of your employers will provide some form of *group life insurance* — it really isn't needed under this scenario but it is usually an inexpensive taxable benefit, so take it!

Starting a Family

When children arrive, you are faced with dependents who are unable to provide for themselves until they are at least age 18. Additionally, a spouse who stays home with the children may also become financially dependent for a period of time. At this time, you may want to consider a small amount of permanent or universal life insurance, with a large amount of term insurance on top.

The universal life policy will provide a base of long-term permanent insurance that will build a cash value that you will always have, and the insurance will also be available for your *estate* to offset any taxes due. Most importantly, a thin layer of insurance purchased at a young age can provide guaranteed insurability throughout life — this may be valuable later in life after a heart attack when you need more insurance, which you otherwise wouldn't be able to purchase. At a young age, permanent insurance of $100,000 should be affordable.

217

But don't buy any more than that — use term insurance for most of your insurance needs at this young age.

For the next 20 years while your children are dependents, purchase about $1.5 million of cheap term insurance for each spouse as temporary protection during this needy period. Note that the exact amount to purchase will depend on your financial *net worth*, your family's cash flow needs without you, and any life insurance coverage already provided by your employer.

Buying a Home

When purchasing a home, a lender often requires you to purchase mortgage insurance as part of the deal. If you own existing life insurance as part of your personal risk management, take steps to have this insurance applied to cover the mortgage specifically, rather than purchasing another small policy as mortgage insurance. Often you don't need a separate policy, so why incur the additional cost?

Emptying the Nest

As you approach age 50 or so, the large amount of term insurance you have starts to get expensive, so get rid of it once the kids have left home and your spouse is back to work. The coverage isn't needed anymore since you are back to a situation where you have no dependents. Better still, you've had 20 years to improve your net worth and build an *RRSP*, and your family is now moving towards self-insurance from a sizable net worth. This means that in case of death, there would be enough personal wealth to support your family.

Approaching Retirement

Seniors in the later years of their career may start to have large amounts of surplus cash flow. Mortgages are now paid off and you are starting to accumulate significant savings outside your *RRSPs*. In these situations, individuals may be able to afford a purchase of universal life insurance for net worth enhancement and to offset taxes on death. A universal policy will build up a cash value that can be yours to borrow against or draw down. A universal policy also offers *tax-sheltered* growth of investment earnings. Keep in mind that the *premiums* can be hefty at this stage, so you need to have a definite cash surplus each year, that you otherwise don't really need, in order to pay the insurance premiums.

Planning Your Estate

When you have strong feelings about tax minimization goals personally or in your estate, or you want to use life insurance to leave specific gifts on your death, universal life insurance, and the deferred buildup of income and gains it can offer, may be suitable for your needs. But unless you are a wealthy senior with surplus cash flow, you likely don't have the resources to consider a sizable policy. If this is the case, I'd much rather see you spend your money to enhance your lifestyle than to buy a life insurance policy that you really don't need, which will only benefit your heirs after you are dead.

See Strategies #42 and #43 for additional discussions on the use of life insurance.

▼

Example

Jean-Paul and Monique have just had their first child, Danielle, and they requested a meeting with their long-time, trusted financial advisor, Sam, in order to consider life insurance needs.

Monique planned to stay home with the baby for about two years, during which time she and the child would be completely financially dependent on Jean-Paul. Jean-Paul did have some group life insurance offered through his employer, but he wanted to ignore it because, "If I leave the company I lose the coverage," and "I have no control over this policy and what it covers." For these reasons, Sam evaluated their life insurance coverage needs assuming they had no coverage currently. Here is what Sam concluded:

Current savings:	$20,000
Current RRSP balance:	$200,000

Value of the home: *not included for this calculation because Monique will need a place in which to live and the home generates no annual income.*

Total investments that could be used to generate income should Jean-Paul die:	**$220,000**

Funeral:	($10,000)
Pay off mortgage:	($180,000)

Taxes on death: none since *assets* transfer
   to spouse tax free
Probate to pay on death: none since all family
assets held legally joint with spouse

Total payments to make on death of Jean-Paul:	**($190,000)**

Investments remaining to provide income to family: **($220,000 less $190,000)**	**$30,000**

Annual pre-tax income required by Monique and baby: $80,000
(assume 80% of current pre-tax income)

Divide by an investment rate of return expected
over the long term in a balanced investment portfolio: ÷7%

Total principal amount needed to generate annual income requirement: **($80,000/0.07)**	**$1,143,000**

Total principal required to generate needed annual income:	$1,143,000
(Less existing assets remaining):	($30,000)
Total additional life insurance required:	**$1,113,000**

Sam concluded that basic term insurance of approximately $1,200,000 is required immediately, and should remain in place for the next 20 years or so. He noted that this amount could be reduced as additional savings are accumulated, or when Monique returns to work. Both of these factors would reduce the amount of insurance needed should Jean-Paul die.

Two Important Notes

1. In calculating the remaining assets that Monique would have to live on, the RRSP has been included with other savings. The RRSP, unlike the other investments, would be fully taxable before it could be spent. For this example, we have assumed that Monique would not live on the RRSP capital (therefore not triggering large amounts of tax) nor any other capital, but would live on the annual income generated by her savings and the insurance proceeds.

2. This example demonstrated the life insurance needs of the family if Jean-Paul were to die. It is important to note that should Monique die first, some insurance coverage may also be needed. Despite the fact that she is not generating an income by working at home, her death would likely mean incremental costs to Jean-Paul in the form of child care, etc. These new costs should be examined in determining the life insurance needs of a stay-at-home spouse.

BONUS
STRATEGY #4

A Roadmap to Your Financial Institution's Investment Products

Today when you visit your bank, credit union, or financial advisor, that institution may bombard you with a myriad of their investment products: traditional *GICs, mutual funds,* wrapped programs, *index* funds, and discretionary accounts. The types of products go on and on, often leaving you overwhelmed by all the choice.

At the other end of the spectrum are financial advisors and institutions that offer only one type of product — their own mutual funds, for example. In these cases, the client has limited choice and often is fitted with these products whether they are the right choice or not.

Many advisors may not be aware of the different types of products to consider for your needs, nor may they be motivated to consider these other products (if they are not financially compensated for them). Also, many advisors and investors immediately focus on specific products, before considering the type of products best suited to your needs. For example, before rushing to buy XYZ Fund, why not think about whether mutual funds in general are best for you?

There are many different types of products and that's what I'd like to explain here.

This strategy will help investors to understand the rainbow of investment products available in the financial institution's inventory today, providing enough information to assist investors to hopefully end up with the types of investment products best suited for them should they choose to stay within the financial institution's array of choices. By no means is my list of options complete — it's only a guide to some of the basics.

Over-the-Counter Investments at Your Financial Institution

At your local bank, trust company, or credit union, a customer service agent can generally offer mutual funds (usually the institution's own funds first), index-linked GICs, GICs, and term deposits to deal with your financial needs. Any more products than that and the customer service agent may need to refer you to an investment specialist or a registered financial advisor. Let's examine these products:

GICs and Index-Linked GICs: In exchange for a lump sum of your money, the bank will pay you a fixed *interest* rate over a period of time typically not exceeding five years. Index-linked GICs modify this return slightly by basing the return you earn on *stock* market returns. Before purchasing either of these instruments, review Strategies #22 and #20. Generally speaking, GICs don't offer the return potential of other fixed income investments available (*bonds*, for example), and index-linked GICs don't offer the tax advantages of investing in real stock market investments using a portion of your money. Examine all the pros and cons of these investments before deciding whether they are a good fit for you.

Bank's Own Mutual Funds: You will likely be exposed to the institution's own mutual funds before any other mutual funds. Mutual funds, in general, will be the best solution for the majority of Canadian investors because of their low investment minimums, broad *diversification* to mitigate *investment risk*, and professional money management on your behalf. Be cautious buying the institution's own funds, however, since these funds are not always the best performers or the most value for your dollar. Consider mutual funds if you have up to $500,000 to invest. Once you have more than that amount, you shouldn't be dealing over the counter with the customer service agent anymore. It's now time for you to explore the institution's *brokerage* services and more sophisticated product lines.

Establishing a Relationship with a Broker at a Brokerage

If you inquire about buying stocks, bonds, or specialty investments like *REITs* or oil and gas royalty *trusts*, you may find your bank/credit union staff referring you to a *broker* at their bank-owned brokerage. Most of the major banks in Canada own their own brokerages, which offer a full array of financial products along with varying levels of investment service. A broker is a full-time investment professional who will proceed to understand your investment needs in detail and build an investment *portfolio* around those needs. A broker may introduce you to Canadian stocks, foreign stocks, all kinds of bonds, mutual funds, GICs, and *wrapped investment products* offered by the brokerage. Each of these products is described elsewhere in the book.

Deciding whether you need to deal with a brokerage at all depends on how much money you have to invest and the amount of time you personally want to commit to your investing. Full-service brokerage service is the most expensive option, because you are hiring an investment advisor to advise you on what to buy, and to help you make the purchase. *Discount brokerage* service is less costly, but there is no advisor to tell you what to buy — instead, you must do your own research, and then the brokerage simply processes your purchase or sell order for a lower fee than the full-service brokerage would.

Once you have more than $500,000 to invest, you should start evaluating *pooled funds* (instead of mutual funds) to take advantage of the cost savings over mutual funds (see Strategy #17). Wrapped pooled programs also make sense at this wealth level. These types of products are generally available from full-service or discount brokerages only.

Once you have $1 million or more to invest, it's time to move from funds and pools into *segregated money management* (see Strategy #18), where you now get ownership of individual stocks and bonds as opposed to owning fund *units* (which is beneficial for tax reasons). With $1 million, an advisor may introduce you to a segregated wrapped program where you can hire several professional *money managers*, each with a different investment mandate. This route leaves the advisor to act as the intermediary and service your needs, free from daily money management responsibilities. Many brokerages have put together segregated wrapped programs to address the need for segregated money management. These programs can be expensive, so negotiate the fee as low as possible and shop around among institutions.

Once you have more than $5 million to invest, you should be dealing with the private client services department of your local institution. With this amount of money to invest, highly trained professional advisors may be exposing you directly to professional money managers who will customize an investment portfolio for you, where you will have direct contact with the money manager. Much of your wealth may be invested around the world, using many of the globe's leading advisors to pick the investments on your behalf. You may or may not have the ability to have any direct involvement in the investment selections, but generally this role will be left to the professional managers. Finally, at this wealth level, your annual fees should be well below 1% per year, based on the large investment amount under management.

In summary, use this chart to evaluate the types of products you should be purchasing:

Investable Amount	Type of Product to Consider within your Financial Institution
$0 to $500,000	Mutual funds
$500,000 to $1 million	Pooled funds; wrapped pooled programs
$1 million to $5 million	Segregated wrapped programs, individual segregated money managers
$5 million plus	Individual stocks and bonds portfolio created by several professional segregated money managers.

Examples

Young Parents with a New Baby Wanting to Open an RESP

An *RESP* or an "in-trust" account generally can be opened over the counter at the financial institution's local branch. Investments such as mutual funds are a logical choice.

A 20-Something Student Starting a First Job After Graduation

If the student is comfortable purchasing the financial institution's own mutual funds, he or she can set up a savings plan for an *RRSP* in a local branch. If the student wants access to the 2,000 or so mutual funds in Canada, he or she may need to move to a brokerage instead of the branch. If the student wants to do his or her own investing, opening a discount brokerage account is an option. If the student wants assistance from an advisor, he or she should consider a full-service brokerage account.

A 40-Year-Old with No Time to Spend on Investing

With a large RRSP starting to accumulate, as well as potential savings beyond the RRSP, the investor should consider full-service brokerage accounts if there is little time to do his or her own investing.

A 40-Year-Old with a Little Time to Play Around with Investments on His or Her Own

Same answer as above, except that the investor in this case should carve off a small amount of money and open a discount brokerage account to dabble in personal investment favourites. The amount of money in this account should not be significant — the serious wealth should be invested by professional money managers.

A 60-Year-Old with More Time to Track Investments

Seniors are at an age where generally they will own more bonds than stocks in their investment portfolios. Market-traded bonds are available through a brokerage account, full-service or discount. Regardless of the large amount of time available to tinker with investing, the senior should limit personal involvement to only the small "play money" account we established above.

Older Senior at Age 70

At this stage in life, I think the investments should be on autopilot, so the senior can relax knowing he or she will get a cheque from his or her *RRIF* each month with no more personal involvement in investing. Use of the bank's full-service brokerage arm will allow the senior to utilize an advisor who will take care of all investing needs.

Important Note

This strategy only discusses some of the services available at financial institutions (particularly banks) specifically. Similar services are available from a variety of other organizations, and you should comparison shop among different types of financial organizations when deciding where to take your business. You may want to consider money management firms, financial planning companies, life insurance companies, and mutual fund agencies, to name just a few.

BONUS STRATEGY #5

Get Your Investment Advisor and Tax Accountant Working Together for You

Separately, neither your investment advisor nor your tax accountant may know enough to manage your wealth effectively, because each may not have the complete financial picture required to integrate planning strategies across investing goals, tax goals, and other goals you have. Together, these advisors have a greater ability to manage your entire financial situation and provide you with financial peace of mind.

Many investment advisors, much like mutual fund managers, are motivated to produce the highest gross return on investment, rather than the after-tax return that matters to you. Taxes have a significant impact on investment returns and investment strategies. Tax is an important variable, albeit only one of many variables, that must be considered in selecting the right investments for your *portfolio*. Keep in mind that the largest expenditure you may make in your lifetime will likely be the payment of income tax.

Understanding the intricacies of income taxes in Canada, one of the highest-taxed nations in the world, is a complex job. The leaders in tax expertise in Canada tend to be tax lawyers and tax chartered accountants who have completed the *CICA* In Depth Course and work full-time in tax consulting. This formal training, supplemented by ongoing work experience and constant upgrading, is the minimum it takes to stay on the leading edge of Canadian taxation.

Now this is not to say that your investment advisor should necessarily be this highly tax trained, although there are some out there who are. However, you should consider the following suggestion: if you have a tax accountant who does your tax return, and if he or she is qualified, ask your accountant to get involved in consulting on the tax effectiveness of your investments and to generally assist you to "kick the tires" of new investment options.

Many of the larger investment *brokerages* in Canada have formal tax specialists on staff providing information to investment advisors about taxation. Your investment advisor likely has access to this information. But using it and understanding it are not the same. By asking some questions based on the content of this book, you may be able to tell if you are dealing with a competent tax advisor. If you are not, find one — and if you are looking for an investment advisor anyway, look for one with tax expertise, or one who recognizes his or her tax limitations and uses outside advisors where necessary. Seeking advice from an investment advisor who claims to have a solid grasp on tax rules but lacks any formal training or experience can be dangerous. Of course, these same rules apply to searching for a tax accountant: seek advice from a tax accountant who is a properly qualified tax advisor.

Overall, making a team out of your investment advisor and tax accountant can be a very powerful tool toward wealth maximization.

BONUS
STRATEGY # 6

Don't Rush to Sell Investments

Throughout time, only a few professional *money managers* have been able to outperform the market consistently. You've heard the names: Peter Lynch, Warren Buffett, Sir John Templeton. These legendary money managers have demonstrated to the world that it is possible to beat the *stock* market by a sizable margin over time. However, it's important to remember that these individuals are the exception, not the rule.

So how did they do it? It's all about management style and sticking, with it. These professional money managers followed their own distinct, well-articulated money management style (growth and value are examples of management style) and philosophy faithfully through good times and bad. As the markets changed, their styles remained the same. They ignored the economic reports on the future, avoided the market confusion, and applied their management styles consistently over time.

These investing heroes have had periods of poor *performance* — not because of a sudden loss of investment savvy, but because the management style they followed so diligently fell out of favour with market conditions of the time. Markets are ever changing, and attempts to predict which management style will be in favour during a particular period have proven to be as difficult as trying to pick a stock winner — it's not easily done, and rarely done consistently.

In Canada, there have been many recent substantial redemptions by investors from Canadian *equity mutual funds* that underperformed the markets last year. Some of these moves are based on a change in the quality of the money manager (change to a new management philosophy that is yet to be proven, internal conflict in the company, loss of key personnel, etc.) and may be clever moves. But some of these moves are simply investors chasing performance — looking for the next star — historically proven very difficult to do. It is unlikely that many of these underperformers have "lost their touch" overnight. Rather, these are often cases of professional managers sticking to their styles while the market changed. If anything, investors should hold onto these funds because of their professionally consistent approach to money management.

What is a management style? Two fundamental management styles are growth and value. A growth money manager purchases the stock of companies that have growing profits and business expansion opportunities, presumably resulting in increasing stock prices. Computer companies are examples of growth stocks. These stocks can soar if conditions are right, but can drop as easily if they don't meet market expectations.

A value money manager purchases stock of companies that appear to be undervalued based on their current *share* price, perhaps because they are out of market favour. Using a value style typically offers tax-effective lower *portfolio* turnover. Value portfolio managers often follow a *buy-and-hold* strategy, often holding a stock 3–5 years, unlike a momentum-based growth manager who may trade more often.

Investment research has tracked the historic results of growth and value management styles, and has provided these important facts:

- Long-term performance has been similar under both growth and value management styles. Short-term performance, however, is significantly affected by management style. When the markets favour a particular style, managers practising this style generally all do well.
- Historically, growth and value styles have different cycles of high and low performance. Predicting when a management style will move into or out of favour is very difficult.

So, What is an Investor to Do?

1. Don't overreact to short-term poor performance. If the same great minds are at the controls, and there have been no significant changes in other key organizational factors, find comfort in knowing that your professional money manager is applying a consistent methodology to investing your money. Once you realize that management style drives performance and no single manager will shine all the time, you'll be less likely to jump ship when a money manager has a bad year or two.

2. Diversify your portfolio with both growth and value management styles. This way, when one style is out of favour, hopefully the other will be in favour, reducing the volatility of investment returns. Since each money manager usually uses only one style, this typically means you should hire at least two separate organizations to manage your money.

3. Beware of owning too many funds. If you own 10 Canadian *equity* funds, you may be incurring significant management fees for what may amount to no more than a broad

index fund. Or you may own eight funds that use the same
management style, which does little to mitigate *investment
risk* — the illusion of *diversification* without the benefits.
Attempting to spread your investment dollars too thinly
may result in a loss of your overall investment objectives.
Organize a disciplined approach to the funds you own,
in each *asset* class, and fill in gaps with new money each
year.

4. Don't forget about the tax impact of selling. If you sell
and trigger a *taxable capital gain*, you will lose a portion of
your investment to tax. Any new investment must have
the return potential to not only match the previous
return expectations, but also generate additional return
to cover the taxes. If the new investment cannot generate
adequate return to cover the lost tax amount, are you
really better off with the new investment?

You will achieve peace of mind in the long term by creating a disciplined and structured investment program using
money managers with a well-thought-out philosophy of
investing. The practice of selling this year's losers hoping to
find next year's winners leaves the fate of your long-term success more to chance than to talent.

▼

Example

Two friends, Simon and Ravi, are active investors and, like so
many others, they are caught up in the excitement of investing and the stock market. Simon is new to investing while
Ravi has spent a lot of time studying market strategies and
how to invest. Recently they got together to talk about the latest economic developments, share tips on hot investments,
and brag about their latest returns.

Both do their own investing. Simon relies on the *mutual fund* returns in the newspapers to pick the latest *hot fund,* and brags he now owns 28 different mutual funds. He was telling Ravi about several brand new funds in the technology sector that he had just bought. He is convinced this area is about to take off because an investment newsletter he reads said so. As well, Simon sold 22 of his funds because of poor performance last year. He is currently sitting in cash, thinking about where to invest next. He likes the high tech sector, and is contemplating putting lots of his money there.

Simon asked Ravi what he thought.

Ravi paused to think, and then asked Simon why he decided to do his own investing. Simon enjoys the task of investing, and thought he would try to manage his own money. With that, Ravi started to educate Simon.

Ravi told Simon that owning 28 funds is over-diversification. As Ravi looked at Simon's portfolio, he could see many funds that were duplicates of others, holding the same investments, and sharing the same investment management style. Ravi explained how effective *diversification* can be achieved with about 10 funds, each carefully selected for its particular management style, or its particular focus on one part of the overall market. Money managers are brought together for the different value that each brings to the portfolio. Such an organized structure will help to mitigate *investment risk.* With 28 funds, Simon owned a smorgasbord of investments, and he was not sure how it all fit together or what his risk level really is.

Ravi outlined to Simon the concept of market timing — where investors or money managers jump in and out of the market trying to find the next big win. The opposite to market timing is a buy-and-hold strategy, where you sit tight through all conditions and benefit from all the ups you will experience from always being in the market. Since the markets generally go up, this strategy tends to outperform market-timers over long periods of time. Ravi suggested to Simon that he should consider taking a longer-term approach to his portfolio, with some market-timing managers and some buy-and-hold managers. Simon should place most of his money with these managers and cease the jumping around between funds. Any jumping around should be limited to a small "play money" portfolio, while the rest is left with the professional managers who have full-time careers focused on making us money.

Ravi also explained his concern about buying new funds that may not have a track record. Be cautious about buying funds where the money manager is new and inexperienced, or where the manager that was responsible for the past great performance has recently left. Investigate far more than performance in the newspapers before buying, including the money manager's investing philosophies, style, company turnover, and other qualitative variables that have led to the successful track record. For it is these organizational variables that will assist the organization to continue to generate successful performance numbers.

As well, Ravi noticed Simon's interest in the high tech sector. High tech, like other specialized areas of investment, should be considered aggressive and more risky than average. Investing in these areas should be limited to a small amount of your overall portfolio, in order to smooth volatility.

Simon listened attentively and then thanked Ravi for the advice. It was clear that he needed to do some more research about investing, and reconsider his bold approach to investing his hard-earned dollars.

BONUS
STRATEGY #7

Build Planning into Your
Tax-Return Preparation

Why is it that individuals seek to pay the least amount of money possible to have their tax returns prepared, even though tax is probably the largest expenditure they will make in their lifetime? Isn't good tax planning worth paying for?

The world of Canadian income taxes is complex, confusing, and always changing. In 1998 alone there were many new pages added to the *Income Tax Act*. Professional tax accountants spend all year long understanding new tax rules and how to use the rules effectively for their clients.

If you do not work with income tax every day, it is difficult to stay on top of all the changes. Failure to take advantage of a *tax deduction* or *tax credit* could result in an inflated tax bill every year as long as you live, and could potentially cost you thousands of dollars during your lifetime.

This strategy is aimed at individuals who complete their own personal tax return every year. While this strategy applauds your hard work, it suggests that you get a little help now and then to ensure that you remain on the right track. A review of the accuracy of your return by a tax specialist and a review for planning opportunities can help to ensure that you are taking advantage of all credits and deductions you are entitled to — today, and as your life changes. It will also determine if there are extra steps you and your family can take to minimize and defer tax.

A qualified tax specialist is not someone who simply prepares tax returns. A qualified tax specialist is an individual trained in the laws of the Income Tax Act of Canada and capable of understanding how the rules can be used to save you tax. It is *tax planning*, not *tax compliance* (return preparation), that can result in tax savings and deferral. Tax planning is where the value is, and is worth a lot more than the mechanical process of completing a return. If you are simply preparing your tax return each year, you may not be doing any tax planning at all!

Consider having a qualified specialist review your tax return every three years. Three years because that is as far back as a taxpayer can normally refile to correct errors or omissions found in the return. If a tax specialist only reviews it, but you still complete it, the cost of hiring the tax professional should be lower. Ask the specialist for tax-planning ideas related to your family, your job, investing, and your estate, as part of the return review. One good strategy could pay for this review over and over again. And if you currently have a tax accountant, consider getting a second opinion from another — just as you would with a doctor.

▼

Example

Susie proudly boasts that she does her own tax return each April, and has done it for the last 15 years. But this year she decided to have a friend who is a *CA* review her 1998 tax return, because she heard there were some significant changes to the Income Tax Act in the last few years and maybe they have affected her. She left the return with him, and after a week they got together to discuss his review. He had some suggestions. Here are two:

- Susie and her husband, Michael, were each claiming their own charitable donations on their respective tax returns. Each was claiming about $200. The accountant told Susie to claim all the donations on one return, since the tax rules provide a higher tax credit on donations in excess of $200 each year. By claiming all the donations on one return, Susie and Michael could increase their federal tax credit from 17% to 29%, because total donations made by an individual that are greater than $200 are credited at a higher rate. This would save them more tax every year.
- Susie and Michael had incurred some substantial medical fees last year due to a medical condition Michael developed. These expenses amounted to $20,000 and hadn't been claimed by Susie when doing their tax returns. The accountant explained that these expenses did qualify as a tax credit and would reduce their tax bill by several thousand dollars this year.

Susie was shocked about the charitable donations tip, as she told the accountant they'd done this for ten years. The CA added that they could go back three years to file adjustments that should generate refunds from the changes they would make. Susie was doubly grateful for the medical expense tip, as this would result in significant additional savings. The $300 visit to the accountant was more than paid for!

BONUS STRATEGY #8

Keep Proper Mutual Fund Records to Minimize Tax

Outside Your RRSP or RRIF

Keeping track of the correct cost of your *mutual funds* is important because it can reduce the amount of tax you pay. This record-keeping can be confusing, however, especially if you are trading frequently.

Owners of mutual funds held outside their *RRSP* or *RRIF* will receive *T3 slips* each spring reporting all *interest, dividends, foreign income* (and non-business tax paid), and *capital gains* distributions from the previous year. Whether you received these *distributions* or had them reinvested automatically, they are included in your income and therefore are taxable.

When the income and capital gains are reinvested to purchase additional units, the total distribution amount is added to the original cost of the mutual fund investment in order to calculate the new cost base. Therefore, the cost base of your investment will consist of your original purchase cost plus any distributions that have been reinvested. Failure to remember to add these taxed distributions to your cost base will result in double taxation of your earnings, since a larger capital gain (due to the understated cost base) will result when the investment is eventually sold.

Inside Your RRSP or RRIF

It is a good idea to maximize the *foreign content* inside your RRSP or RRIF since global investment *diversification* can serve to reduce your overall *investment risk*. RRSP/RRIF foreign content limits are based on the cost of investments inside the RRSP or RRIF: only 20% of the cost of all investments can be foreign property.

It is therefore in your best interest to increase the Canadian investment cost base in order to maximize the permissible foreign content. This can be accomplished by regularly selling and repurchasing Canadian *equity* investments that have increased in value inside your RRSP or RRIF and reinvesting foreign equity distributions in Canadian investments, since the gains (both Canadian and foreign) will be added to the cost base of Canadian investments and total investments. This will permit you to purchase additional foreign investments in your RRSP or RRIF. Watch those transaction fees, though!

Finally, here is a word of caution about account transfers. If you have recently transferred an RRSP/RRIF account *in kind* from one institution to another, I suggest you go back and ensure that the receiving institution picked up the correct cost bases to calculate the foreign content limit. The new institution may have incorrectly used the *fair market value* of investments at the time of transfer, rather than the purchase costs, as the new base to calculate the foreign content limit. This can lead to an overstatement or understatement of your permissible foreign content limit depending on your particular situation. An overstatement of the limit could result in penalties from Revenue Canada, while an understatement could unnecessarily reduce your ability to invest outside Canada.

▼

Example

Meghan owned an *equity mutual fund,* which her parents had purchased for her 10 years ago as an education fund. They had invested the proceeds of a gift Meghan had received from non-resident grandparents, and all the fund's income was reinvested in additional fund *units.* In each of those 10 years, Meghan received a T3 slip for dividends earned on the fund and included this dividend income on her tax return.

Six months ago, at age 24, Meghan sold the equity fund in order to use the proceeds to fund her education. Now it's time to do her personal tax return and she has been wondering what the tax implications of the sale are. She visited her father's tax accountant for advice. The tax accountant informed Meghan that she would have to pay tax on a capital gain resulting from the sale, since the fund had significantly appreciated in value. The amount of the capital gain would be the proceeds from the sale less the cost base less any transaction fees. The cost base consisted of the original cost of all fund purchases, plus any distributions received that had been reinvested.

Together, Meghan and the tax accountant reviewed Meghan's income from the mutual fund over the last 10 years. They added up the income from the fund and all of the new purchases to produce a total. The tax accountant told Meghan that this total is the *adjusted cost base,* which is used on her tax return for this year. She should deduct this cost base from the sale proceeds to calculate the capital gain. She should also remember to deduct any load fees and other transaction costs she may have incurred to buy or sell the fund. She should then multiply the remaining capital gain by 75% to produce the taxable capital gain that is reported on page one of the jacket of her tax return and included in her *taxable income.* (Revenue Canada only taxes three-quarters of a capital gain.)

Meghan found the experience with the accountant to be a lesson for the future. She learned that whenever she buys mutual funds outside an RRSP, the accounting for the funds can be confusing and time consuming. Additional purchases and switching between funds can make it even more complicated. However, keeping track of the correct mutual fund costs is important in order to ensure that no additional tax is paid on the eventual sale of the funds.

Crunching the Numbers

The tax accountant and Meghan calculated her cost base and the capital gain of the fund she sold, as follows:

Original purchase amount, 10 years ago: **$10,000**

Annual distributions of dividends (taxed in the year received, and reinvested when received):

Year	Distribution ($)
1	500
2	505
3	515
4	508
5	0
6	460
7	550
8	555
9	555
10	0

(the fund was sold early in year ten)

Total cost base

    (original price plus tax-paid distributions): $14,148

Proceeds on sale: $16,000

Broker's fees incurred to sell: $160

Capital gain: ($16,000 − $14,148) − $160 = $1,692

Taxable capital gain: **$1,692 x 75% = $1,269**

GLOSSARY

Commonly Used Financial Terms

Accrued Capital Gain — An unrealized gain that has been created by the increase in value of an investment or other asset. The excess of market value over adjusted cost base. An accrued gain is a gain that exists before the investment is sold, or deemed sold, to realize the gain.

Accrued Tax Liability — An unrealized tax liability relating to an accrued capital gain. The tax liability continues to accrue as the accrued capital gain increases. This liability will become taxes payable when the investment is eventually sold, or deemed sold, and the gain is realized.

Active Management — Management of, for example, mutual funds by professional money managers who actively buy and sell investments in an attempt to produce a greater rate of return than the market does. The opposite of passive management.

Adjusted Cost Base — The cost of an asset used in computing the capital gain or capital loss on disposition. The purchase price of an asset, plus or minus any adjustments under the Income Tax Act. Generally includes any transaction fees associated with the purchase and reinvested income and capital gains in mutual funds and pooled funds.

After-Tax Rate of Return — A measure of the profit retained from an investment over a period of time, after paying the related income tax. The rate of return is expressed as a percentage.

Allowable Capital Loss — See capital loss.

Annuity — An investment that guarantees a series of payments (often fixed) over a period of time. The amount of the payments can vary according to a number of variables, including interest rates, term, adjustments for inflation, and the price of the annuity.

Asset — Anything with value, either tangible or intangible, owned by an individual or a company. Examples: investments, real estate, vehicles, patents.

Asset Allocation Mix — The division of asset holdings among a variety of categories such as stocks or equity, bonds or fixed income, real estate, cash, etc. Determining a proper asset allocation mix for investing purposes can involve an assessment of one's risk tolerance, need for liquidity, and other factors to create an asset mix consistent with the investor's needs.

Asset Turnover — A measure of the rate of buying and selling of investments in an investment portfolio. Frequent buying and selling by a stock investment manager is high asset turnover.

Attribution Rules — Rules in the Income Tax Act of Canada designed to prevent transferring of investment income between family members for purposes of reducing income taxes paid on that income. The application of these rules results in the taxation of the income in the hands of the transferor.

Average Cost Base — An accounting of the cost of an asset where the owner holds a number of identical units. For example, if you buy 10 units at $20 each, the total cost is $200. If you purchase 10 more units at $30 each, their total cost is $300. You now have 20 units for a total cost of $500 and an average cost per unit of $25 ($500/20).

Balanced Fund — A mutual fund that invests in a mixture of preferred and common stock and bonds, blending income from dividends and interest with long-term growth from stocks.

Bankrupt — The legal status of an insolvent person who has made an assignment of assets in favour of creditors or of a person against whom a receiving order has been made.

Beneficiary — An individual who is entitled to receive assets from a will, funds from a trust, the proceeds from an RRSP or RRIF, the proceeds from a life insurance policy, or some other form of receipt.

Blue Chip Stock — Stock in large, diversified, established companies that may be better able to weather a poor economy than smaller companies.

Bond — A financial contract between an issuer and holder where the issuer promises to pay interest to the holder at specified intervals and a fixed amount at maturity.

Bond Fund — See fixed income fund.

Broker — An investment advisor who is responsible for providing investment advice and executing buy and sell orders on behalf of clients.

Brokerage — An investment firm licensed to buy and sell public securities and other investments.

Buy and Hold — An investment strategy of purchasing an investment with the intent to hold it for several years. The opposite of an investment strategy of frequent buying and selling.

CA — See chartered accountant.

Call Option — An option contract that gives a purchaser the right, but not the obligation, to purchase an investment at a fixed price up to a point in the future.

Canada Pension Plan (CPP) — A retirement savings plan operated by the federal government of Canada. Working Canadians (employees and self-employed individuals) contribute to the plan and in retirement receive benefits in the form of regular payments.

Canadian Controlled Private Corporation (CCPC) — A Canadian corporation that is not controlled by non-residents or public companies or any combination of these types of shareholders. Usually these companies are owned and controlled by Canadian resident individuals or other CCPCs. Unlike a public company, a CCPC is not listed on a public stock exchange. Its stock does not trade publicly.

Canadian Deposit Insurance Corporation (CDIC) — An organization established by the federal government to provide a basic level of deposit insurance to Canadians invested with member institutions. Members include many of the major financial institutions in Canada. CDIC insurance covers bank accounts and GICs but not mutual funds.

Canadian Institute of Chartered Accountants (CICA) — The national association of chartered accountants in Canada. A body that governs and educates chartered accountants in Canada and enforces a strict ethical code on their conduct.

Canadian Resident — For Canadian income tax purposes, an individual who ordinarily resides in Canada (which is a question of fact), or has sojourned in Canada in a particular year by having spent 183 days or more in Canada in that year. A Canadian resident is taxed on his or her worldwide income. As it is possible to be a resident of Canada and another country at the same time under each country's respective tax law, Canada has entered into tax treaties with many countries to prevent double taxation by determining one country of residency and specifying in which of the countries the various sources of income may be taxed.

Canadian Shareholder's Association — An association that educates investors about investing and gives interested investors low-cost access to investing in companies in North America that permit direct stock purchases and dividend reinvestment.

Capital Gain — The excess of the sale proceeds of an asset over its adjusted cost base. A taxable capital gain is 75% of net capital gains (capital gains minus capital losses for the year). A taxable capital gain is the amount you include in income on your tax return.

Capital Loss — The opposite of a capital gain. Seventy-five percent of net capital losses (capital losses minus capital gains) constitute an allowable capital loss. Net capital losses can only reduce taxable capital gains; they cannot otherwise reduce your income. An allowable capital loss can be deducted against past and future taxable capital gains. It can also be carried back up to three years or carried forward indefinitely to be applied against taxable capital gains in other years.

Capped Fund — A fund that is not accepting new investment money. The fund is said to be closed off to new investment.

Cash Position — A strategy in which professional money managers hold a portion of an investment portfolio in cash investments in order to take advantage of future buying opportunities and to cover ongoing liquidity needs. The size of the cash position may vary significantly between managers.

CDIC — See Canadian Deposit Insurance Corporation.

Certified Financial Planner (CFP) — A professional designation offered by the Canadian Association of Financial Planners to individuals who have completed an educational requirement and achieved a level of experience in practising financial planning. The CFP designation is becoming widely recognized as the designation of choice for financial planners in Canada.

CFP — See Certified Financial Planner.

Chartered Accountant (CA) — A Canadian professional accounting designation. One of the world's most recognized and highly regarded professional designations for advising on a broad array of personal and business issues.

CICA — See Canadian Institute of Chartered Accountants.

Clone — A similar copy. To clone a mutual fund is to create a new mutual fund with similar, but not necessarily exactly the same, investment holdings and fees as the original fund. Cloned funds may have higher expenses.

Closed-End Trust — A trust with a fixed number of units for sale. Compare this with a mutual fund trust, which can offer an unlimited number of units for sale to investors as new money is invested with the fund company. Closed-end trust units are sold on a public stock exchange.

Collateral — Any assets pledged to support a debt. These assets may be sold to repay the debt if the borrower defaults on payments on the debt.

Commission — A broker's or agent's fee for executing a buy or sell order for investments owned by a client.

Common Shares or Stock — Stock, issued by a company, representing equity or ownership in the company. The purchaser of the stock is called a shareholder. Common stock usually has voting rights attached and may pay dividends.

Corporation — A legal entity, separate from its owners, through which an incorporated business is operated. A corporation is owned by shareholders. A corporation is also referred to as a company.

CPP — See Canada Pension Plan.

Crystallization — The recognition for tax purposes of an increase in value of an investment without a sale. If you had an accrued gain in a stock on February 22, 1994, you were permitted to apply your remaining personal $100,000 capital gains exemption against some portion of this accrued gain, in effect crystallizing or realizing a gain for tax purposes and offsetting it with your exemption. The crystallized gain would have increased the cost base of the investment. Such a crystallization has a benefit when the stock is eventually sold, since any future gain should be smaller because of the higher cost base. A similar mechanism exists for mutual funds, whereby exempt capital gains balances, created by accrued capital gains in existence on February 22, 1994, can be used to offset future capital gains.

Deemed Disposition — A notional disposition (not a real sale) of an asset resulting in a realization of any accrued capital gains or losses and triggering any resulting tax. A deemed disposition occurs, for example, upon a death, when the deceased's assets are deemed to be disposed of at fair market value and tax may be due on any gains realized.

Deferral of Tax — The process of delaying the payment of tax until a point in the future. RRSPs and RRIFs defer tax since no tax is paid on income earned in the plan until the proceeds are withdrawn (usually in retirement). Deferral of tax is desirable because it permits assets to continue to earn income on a pre-tax basis, enhancing the growth rate.

Deferred Load — A deferred sales charge on mutual funds that occurs on the selling of the fund, rather than on its purchase. Also called a back-end load. Deferred loads or sales charges usually decrease to zero over a set period of years.

Depreciation — A notional charge against a capital asset to recognize that an asset's value is eroded with use over time. A non-cash expense that may be tax deductible (with very specific rules) for individuals and businesses. See also recapture.

Derivative — A financial instrument, such as an option or future contract, that derives its value from another asset or investment. For example, an option contract to buy Coca Cola stock at a future date for a fixed price is a derivative. If the value of the stock goes up, so does the value of the option. On that future date, if the market price of Coke stock is greater than the option, the derivative holder can exercise the option, purchase Coke shares at the fixed price, then sell those shares at the higher market price, and profit on the difference. Or the holder could sell the option for a profit, since the value of the option would increase if the underlying stock could be purchased for a profit.

Disability Insurance — Insurance that protects against the loss of income of the insured individual because of illness or accident.

Discount Brokerage — A company, or division of a bank, that sells financial products with lower fees than a full-service investment brokerage but provides little personal assistance and no advice to clients. Discount brokers assist clients to execute their transactions.

Discretionary Account — A discretionary account is an investment portfolio in which the financial advisor can buy and sell securities on the client's behalf without client approval. See also non-discretionary account.

Disposition — The act of parting with something, whether it be a sale, gift, loss, or destruction. Also called disposal.

Distribution — Money allocated or directed to a unit holder of a mutual or pooled fund. A distribution may be interest, dividends, capital gains, or foreign income.

Diversification — The process of investing in a variety of countries, industries, and asset classes, across fixed income maturities and quality of debt, and across management styles, in order to reduce risk of loss. A loss in one particular area would have a limited impact on the overall portfolio because of diversification.

Dividend — An after-tax corporate distribution paid to shareholders. Dividends may or may not be paid regularly, and the amount paid may vary. Dividends are generally subject to the lowest rate of tax on any type of investment income in Canada.

Dividend Reinvestment Plan — An arrangement whereby an owner reinvests dividend income for additional purchase of the original investment. Dividend reinvestment plans operate like compound interest and can permit much faster growth of investments because of the potential to earn income on income.

Downsizing — Moving from something larger to something smaller.

Earned Income — A term used for tax purposes that generally includes total income from employment and self-employment, alimony receipts, and rental income. Earned income is reduced by losses in self-employment, and rental losses. Earned income is important in determining RRSP contribution limits.

ECGB — See exempt capital gains balance.

Emerging Market Bond — A bond offered by a second- or third-world country. Emerging market countries are countries that offer great opportunities (with greater risk) for development and industrialization and are eager to develop their economies.

Employment Income — Salary, wages, tips, gratuities, bonuses, and other benefits received in relation to a job. Annual employment income is reported to you on form T4, which is received from your employer each tax season.

Equity — Stock issued by a company, representing ownership in that company. See also stock; equity mutual fund.

Equity Mutual Fund — A mutual fund investing in equities or stocks of companies. There are several categories of equity mutual funds, including Canadian and international, among others.

Estate — The sum of the value of all an individual's property. All assets and liabilities owned by an individual at the time of his or her death.

Estate Freeze — The process of crystallizing the value of an individual's assets, typically the value of a business interest at its current market value, for tax purposes. This facilitates the transfer of future growth in the business at a low tax cost to other family members.

Estate Planning — The process of making legal and financial decisions relating to an individual's assets that will apply after death. Planning may involve preparing a will, creating a trust, implementing powers of attorney, and picking an estate executor, among other responsibilities.

Executor — A party named by an individual to carry out the provisions of his or her will.

Exempt Capital Gains Balance (ECGB) — A notional account representing the capital gain realized from the capital gains election made for flow through entities such as mutual funds. ECGB may have been created with the filing of your 1994 tax return. In that return you were permitted to create an account or pool consisting of the amount by which mutual fund market values exceeded the cost base on February 22, 1994. These accounts are available to reduce future capital gains distributed by the mutual fund or capital gains resulting from the sale of the mutual fund units, and effectively reduces any gains to zero for tax purposes, until the ECGB account is reduced to nil. ECGB accounts exist separately for each qualifying mutual fund.

Exercise — To assert a right in relation to a company stock option: to act on the option, advising the company that you would like to acquire the stock available from exercising the option.

Exercise Price — The price at which the owner of a stock option is entitled to purchase a share of the stock. Also called a strike price.

Face Value — The value of a bond that appears on its certificate. This is usually the amount to be received on maturity, excluding any interest income.

Fair Market Value — The amount that a buyer and seller would agree on in relation to the purchase and sale of an item, where the market is unrestricted and the buyer and seller are not connected in any way.

Financial Planner — A qualified individual who assists clients with the process of financial planning.

Financial Planning — A process of developing and prioritizing financial goals, and developing strategies to meet those goals. The process involves collecting information about a client's current personal and financial situation, identifying goals, developing alternatives and recommendations to meet goals, providing assistance with implementing goals, and monitoring the client's achievement of those goals over time.

Fixed Income Fund — A mutual fund that invests primarily in bonds, mortgages, and/or other forms of debt. Bond funds are a form of fixed income fund.

Foreign Content — The portion of an investment portfolio that is invested outside Canada. For an individual's RRSP, the foreign content is restricted to 20% of the book value or cost.

Foreign Income — Income earned from sources outside Canada. For tax purposes, foreign investment income, including dividends (but excluding capital gains), is taxed as regular income.

Formal Trust — A legal relationship, evidenced by an agreement, created when a person (settlor) transfers property to another (trustee) who is responsible for dealing with the property for the benefit of persons known as beneficiaries. The fundamental characteristic of a trust is the separation of management of the property from entitlement to it. A trust is a separate taxpayer and must file a tax return annually.

Front-End Load — A fee paid on the purchase of a mutual fund. See also deferred load.

Full-Service Investment Advisor — An advisor that sells financial products and provides a broad array of financial advice and services to clients who don't have the time, knowledge, experience, or desire to select and manage their own investments.

Fund Company — A company that offers mutual funds for sale. Mutual fund companies may also sell other services and products such as segregated money management or pooled funds.

Fund Manager — A professional money manager who is responsible for selecting and timing the purchase and sale of investments in a portfolio. A fund manager can be an individual, a team of individuals, or a company.

Future — A contract that requires its owner to buy or sell a certain financial instrument at a stated price by a specified date.

GIC — See guaranteed investment certificate.

Global Diversification — The process of investing around the world to reduce the risk that significant loss in any one country would have a large impact on a portfolio of investments. See also diversification.

Goods and Services Tax (GST) — A federal tax of 7% on the consumption of goods and services in Canada. The tax is collected by businesses on certain goods and services for sale.

Group Life Insurance — Life insurance provided through an employer for an employee group. While this insurance can be quite inexpensive, the coverage may not suit your needs and may not be fully transferable if you leave the employer.

GST — See Goods and Services Tax.

Guaranteed Investment Certificate (GIC) — A fixed income investment in which an investor deposits funds in an institution like a bank for a specified period of time and the institution pays the investor a fixed rate of return on the investment over that period. Principal is repaid to the investor at the end of that term. The investment return is in the form of interest income and the investment is usually locked in for its agreed term.

Higher-Tax-Rate Income — Income that attracts a higher rate of tax depending on the taxpayer's marginal tax bracket.

Hot Fund — A fund for which the money manager has produced some very good returns recently or over the long term, compared to similar investments. See also star manager.

In Kind — As is. Transferring an investment whole, without selling it. Simply moving the existing investment to another institution or plan.

Income Tax Act of Canada — The federal statute that contains the income tax laws and regulations governing the taxation of individuals, corporations, and trusts in Canada. Such laws are created and amended federally by the minister of finance. Revenue Canada is the federal government department that administers the Income Tax Act and deals with Canadians and their federal taxes.

Income Trust — An investment structured as a trust that invests in income-producing assets, such as resource properties (oil, gas, and mining) or businesses, where the revenues, net of expenses, are distributed to investors.

Index — A market indicator of broad market performance. In Canada, the Toronto Stock Exchange Composite Index (also called the TSE 300 Composite Index) includes stocks of 300 large and established Canadian companies. In the U.S., the Standard & Poor's 500 index (S&P 500) comprises 500 U.S. companies that are representative of all industry groups.

Index Mutual Fund — A mutual fund that invests in the same securities included in a broad market index like the TSE 300 Composite in Canada or the Standard & Poor's 500 in the United States. This type of fund has no active fund manager, since its holdings try to mirror the index and produce a rate of return similar to the index.

Inflation — A measure of the increase in cost of living over time. An example of the impact of inflation has been the rising price of a postage stamp over the years. As the cost of living increases through inflation, your income must also grow, in order to prevent a decrease in your standard of living through a loss of purchasing power.

Informal "In-Trust" Account — An "in-trust" arrangement offered by many Canadian financial institutions and investment brokerages, under which funds are held in trust by a parent (the trustee) for a child but a formal trust with related documentation is not created.

Insolvent — Being unable to pay debts as they become due.

Interest — The cost of borrowing a sum of money or the benefit for lending a sum of money. Usually computed as a percentage rate over time.

International Equity Mutual Fund — A stock-based mutual fund that invests in the stock of companies based outside Canada.

Investment Income — Income earned on passive investment of capital, such as interest, dividends, and capital gains. Investments can include stocks, bonds, GICs, mutual funds, rental properties, and pooled funds, among others.

Investment Risk — The risk that an investment will not provide the return expected, or that the investment will lose money.

Joint and Last to Die — A characteristic of a life insurance policy where the proceeds of the policy will be paid out to the beneficiaries only on the death of the last spouse. Having a policy that pays out on the death of the second spouse is usually less expensive to purchase than a policy on the life of one of the spouses. This type of policy would not be useful to a family where the surviving spouse could not support his/her lifestyle without the insurance proceeds.

Joint Ownership — Ownership of an asset by two or more people, where each person has an undivided interest in the property. Joint ownership can permit any owner to have access to the asset either on their own or together with the other joint owners.

Labour Fund — A labour-sponsored venture capital corporation is a type of investment offering yet another asset class for a diversified portfolio: venture capital. Labour funds, which operate much like mutual funds, have been approved by the federal and provincial governments for the purposes of making investments into private businesses in Canada. See also venture capital.

Leverage — The act of borrowing money to invest.

Life Insurance — A financial safety net where under a policy contract you pay specified amounts (premiums) to an insurance company and in exchange the insurance company agrees to pay your estate or family a lump-sum amount when you die. The amount of your premiums is based on a number of variables, including how much insurance you want, your age, health condition, whether you smoke, your sex, etc. The policy payout is based on the terms of the policy and can be structured by the insurance company to be tax free when paid.

Life Insurance Segregated Funds — Seg funds are like mutual funds in that they are an investment fund that offers growth and income potential but, unlike mutual funds, they have characteristics of an insurance product: they are offered through insurance companies. When purchasing a seg fund, you're buying an insurance contract, a variable deferred annuity, which comes with certain guarantees. The contract is governed by provincial life insurance regulations.

Line of Credit — An agreement under which a lender of

money agrees to provide funds to a borrower as needed by the borrower, up to a fixed limit. The lender charges interest on the amount borrowed.

Liquidity — The ease with which an investment can be converted into cash.

Load — A transaction charge on the purchase or sale of units of a mutual fund. Loads can be front-end or deferred (or rear-end, also called deferred sales charges).

Locked-in Investment — An investment you are unable to convert into cash until a point in time agreed upon when the investment was purchased. GICs may be locked in for one year, for example.

Management Expense — A fee paid for the operation and administration of a mutual fund or other managed investment account. This is different from a load or a trailer, or a commission. The management fee for a mutual fund can include payment for the managers' salaries, advertising costs, and other administrative costs of operating the fund company and its funds.

Management Expense Ratio (MER) — A representation of all costs of operating a fund, including management expenses, expressed as a percentage of the net assets of the fund. For example, a typical Canadian equity mutual fund might charge a management expense ratio of around 2.25% annually.

Marginal Tax Rate — The tax rate that applies to the next dollar of taxable income you earn, given a specific taxable income level. Knowing your marginal tax rate for different types of income can permit you to organize your income sources to reduce tax paid.

Market Capitalization — A measure of the dollar value of a company. The total number of shares multiplied by the current price per share.

MER — See management expense ratio.

Money Manager — A person, group of people, or company

that handles investments on behalf of others. The manager may buy or sell investments on behalf of the investors.

Money Market Instrument — A short-term fixed income investment. Examples include Treasury bills, GICs, money market mutual funds, and short-term bonds.

Mortgage — A legal contract, relating to a loan between a borrower and lender, where the lender receives the right to own pledged property if the borrower does not meet the conditions outlined in the loan agreement.

Mutual Fund — A professionally managed pool of investments owned by a group of investors. An investor can buy units in a fund and effectively invest in a wide range of stocks, bonds, and other investments that he or she might otherwise not be able to afford. Many funds are legally structured as trusts or corporations, and the income earned by the fund each year is distributed to the unit holders after expenses are deducted for managing and operating the fund. Investors can purchase mutual funds that invest in bonds, stocks, and other instruments in Canada and many other countries in the world.

Mutual Fund Corporation — A corporation set up by a mutual fund company, where different classes of shares are issued to represent investment in different types of mutual funds. Unit holders can switch among funds inside the corporation and not realize capital gains. But these funds are tax deferred, not tax exempt. This means that when the shares are eventually redeemed from the corporation, income tax will be due on the accumulated capital gains.

Natural Index Fund — A fund that replicates an index by purchasing the underlying investments that compose the index. For a Canadian equity index fund, the fund manager might purchase the stock of corporations included in the TSE 300 in the same proportion reflected in the index.

Net Asset Value — The value of one unit or share of a mutual fund. The total market value of all investments owned by a mutual fund, less all liabilities, divided by the number of units outstanding.

Net Capital Loss — See capital loss.

Net Worth — The difference between the value of an individual's total assets and his or her total liabilities. The improvement of an individual's net worth over time is a measure of success in personal finance.

No-Load Fund — A mutual fund that has no purchase or sale fees.

Non-Discretionary Account — A non-discretionary account is an investment portfolio in which the financial advisor must obtain client approval for each trade completed in the portfolio. See also discretionary account.

Non-Registered Investment — An investment that is not tax sheltered because it is held outside a registered plan such as a registered retirement savings plan or registered retirement income fund. Also called a non-RRSP/RRIF investment. Income from non-registered investments is subject to tax.

Non-RRSP/RRIF — See non-registered investment.

Notional Disposition — See deemed disposition.

Offshore Trust — A trust established and operated outside Canada. See also formal trust.

Option Contract — An instrument representing the right to buy or sell an investment at an agreed-upon price known as the strike price. See also call option; put option.

Passive Management — Management that is associated with index mutual funds, where no professional money management is used but rather investments are purchased and sold to match the index that the fund is trying to mirror. The opposite of active management.

Pension Plan — A registered retirement plan sponsored by an employer for the benefit of employees. A pension plan is subject to government regulation and can be either a defined benefit plan or a defined contribution plan. Contributions to a pension plan may be made by employers and employees and are generally tax deductible. Growth inside the plan is tax sheltered until the benefits are paid out to a pensioner in retirement.

Performance — A measure of the success of an investment according to its increase in value and/or income generated over a period of time. Also called (percentage) rate of return on an investment.

Personal Rate of Return — A measure of the performance of an investment for the period of time that the investor owned the investment, instead of a period of time determined on some other basis like a calendar year.

Pooled Fund — A fund investment similar to a mutual fund, except that in this case minimum investment amounts are $150,000 and MERs tend to be much lower than those of mutual funds. See also mutual fund.

Portfolio — The collection of investments held by an investor, whether registered or non-registered.

Premium — The purchase price of ownership of an amount of life insurance. Premiums can be paid in a lump sum or, more commonly, over a period of time.

Prescribed Annuity — An annuity that provides the beneficiary with a consistent stream of receipts over a future period of time. The payments consist of principal and interest. A prescribed annuity provides interest income evenly over the annuity's term, unlike a regular annuity, which provides interest income in decreasing amounts over the term of the annuity. A prescribed annuity serves to defer taxation better than a regular annuity because of the deferral of payment of interest over the life of the annuity.

Pre-Tax Return — A measure of the performance of an investment before related income tax is considered. Pre-tax or gross return is the return you see in the newspaper and what your advisor may report to you. These returns may or may not be after the payment of any fees, as well.

Probate Fee — A provincial fee, not a tax, for the processing or validation of a will for a deceased individual. Probate fees vary by province. They are calculated based on the value of assets in an estate.

Prospectus — A legal document outlining the key information about a particular investment. A prospectus is provided by the investment product offerer when the investment is offered for sale to the public. Prospectuses should be presented to and discussed with clients prior to the purchase of investments. Prospectuses for mutual funds contain information on fund fees, objectives, and administrative matters, among other things.

Public Corporation — A company whose stock is listed and traded on a public stock exchange in Canada. Because public stock is bought and sold on a public exchange, ownership can be more widely held and stock can usually be traded more easily.

Purchasing Power — A measure of the amount of goods and services that can be bought today with a given sum, compared to a prior or future period. A measure of how much a dollar buys over time. Purchasing power is eroded by inflation, which raises prices and reduces how much a dollar will buy.

Put Option — An option contract that gives a purchaser the right, but not the obligation, to sell an investment at a fixed price at a point in time in the future.

Real Estate Investment Trust (REIT) — A publicly traded closed-end trust that owns, operates, acquires, and develops or finances real estate properties.

Realization of a Gain — Receipt of the benefit of an increase in the value of an investment (gain) by its actual or deemed sale. Before the gain is realized, the gain is accruing on

1

the investment. Capital gains are taxable only when they are realized, not when they are accruing.

Recapture — The difference between the lesser of the cost or sales price of a depreciable asset and the remaining tax cost (after depreciation). This difference is taxed as regular income. The excess of the sale price over the cost is taxed as a capital gain.

Redemption Charge — A fee charged to an investor for selling an investment within a predetermined time after the purchase. Also called a deferred load for mutual funds.

Registered Education Savings Plan (RESP) — A savings plan registered with the federal government that allows contributions to accumulate and grow on a tax-deferred basis for the purpose of funding post-secondary education costs of named beneficiaries. Contributions are not tax deductible. Withdrawals by the child for eligible educational purposes in the future will be taxable in the hands of the child (likely little or no tax).

Registered Retirement Income Fund (RRIF) — An individual retirement account registered with the federal government. The assets have been transferred in from an RRSP or registered pension plan. Contributions cannot be made to a RRIF, and the annuitant must withdraw minimum sums from the RRIF each year according to government-determined amounts. Payments made out of the plan are taxable. Funds inside the RRIF can continue to be invested as desired and remain tax deferred until withdrawn. There are no maximum withdrawal amounts. An individual can convert an RRSP to a RRIF at any age up to but no later than the year in which he or she turns 69.

Registered Retirement Savings Plan (RRSP) — A savings or investment plan registered with the federal government of Canada. Contributions to RRSPs are based on limits determined with reference to earned income and benefits accruing under employer-sponsored registered pension plans and deferred profit-sharing plans. Contributions are tax deductible, and income inside the plan grows tax deferred. Individuals can contribute to their own RRSP or to a spousal RRSP. With a spousal RRSP, the contributor gets the tax deduction and the spouse withdraws the investment at least three years in the future and pays tax on the withdrawals at that time.

Regular Income — Income other than investment income. Includes employment, business, and rental income. This is income that is not taxed at a preferred lower tax rate such as that applicable to dividends and capital gains. In Canada, foreign investment income may also be taxed as regular income.

REIT — See real estate investment trust.

RESP — See registered education savings plan.

Retiring Allowance — A payment, for lengthy service or termination, for example, to an employee leaving an employer due to either retirement or forced early departure.

Revenue Canada — The federal government department that administers and enforces the laws contained in the Income Tax Act.

Risk/Return Balance — The trade-off between an individual's risk tolerance and his or her expected return on investment. Usually, the higher the potential rate of return, the higher the risk associated with getting this return.

Risk Tolerance — A measure of an individual's willingness or ability to endure risk — the possibility of a decline in the value of investments — in an attempt to obtain higher investment returns.

RRIF — See registered retirement income fund.

RRSP — See registered retirement savings plan.

RRSP Contribution — An amount of money or the value of an asset deposited in an RRSP. The deposit amount is limited (as discussed under registered retirement savings plan). An individual's contribution may not necessarily match the tax deduction for the year; the individual can contribute to an RRSP and defer taking the tax deduction until the future.

Segregated Money Management — The management of an investor's money and portfolio separate from other investors, where each investor owns their own portfolio of stocks and bonds. This differs from the situation in a mutual fund, where investors own units in a pool and never own individual securities directly.

Self-Employment Income — Income earned through an unincorporated business or professional practice. A doctor or lawyer in private practice usually earns self-employment income.

Share — A representation of ownership or equity of a company or corporation. See also stock.

Share Purchase Program — An agreement whereby a company offers investors the opportunity to purchase additional stock directly from the company.

Sole Proprietorship — An unincorporated business owned by one person. An unincorporated business is not separate from its owner, and therefore there is no need to file a separate tax return for the business. Rather, the net income of the business is included on the tax return of the owner.

Star Manager — A mutual fund manager or other professional money manager who is very good at managing money and producing above-average rates of return for investors over a period of time.

Stock — A representation of equity ownership of a company or corporation. Stock can be common or preferred. Each type of stock has different rights attached, such as voting ability and dividend entitlement.

Stock Exchange — A marketplace for buying and selling investments. A place where stock of public companies is listed and traded. Examples of stock exchanges include the Toronto Stock Exchange and the New York Stock Exchange.

Stock Option — A financial instrument given to an employee that permits the employee to purchase company shares at a specified price (exercise price) within a specified time period.

Street Name — A security registered in "street name" is a fully negotiable instrument to anyone who possesses the security. Brokerages will hold client securities in street name (rather than the client's name) to facilitate ease of transfer, buying and selling on behalf of the client.

Strike Price — See exercise price.

Stripped Bond — A bond from which the interest payments ("coupons") have been removed. The remaining residue is then sold at a discount to its face value and matures at face value. The coupons are also sold at a discount to maturity value. The term "stripped bond" has come to reflect both the residual bond and the coupon payments.

Synthetic Index Fund — A fund that may use derivatives to purchase exposure to a particular index. A synthetic fund may use a futures contract to provide investors with a rate of return equal to the change in the index.

Tax Bracket — A specified range of taxable income to which a given tax rate applies. In Canada, tax rates are progressive; that is, the rate of tax generally increases as income increases.

Tax Compliance — The process of reporting tax information required by statute, including completing a tax return. This differs from tax planning, which provides strategies to save and defer tax.

Tax Credit — An amount that is applied directly to reduce the amount of tax owing by an individual, trust, or company in preparing its tax return. This differs from a tax deduction, which reduces the amount of income that is subject to tax.

Tax Deduction — A deduction from the amount of income that is subject to tax, resulting in a reduction of the amount of tax owing by an individual, trust, or company.

Tax Instalment — The amount of tax remitted by a taxpayer to Revenue Canada on a quarterly basis (in the case of individuals). Individuals are required to make tax instalments if they earn a large amount of income from which no tax is withheld at source. Tax instalments can be calculated according to three methods, and the method most appropriate to you should be determined.

Tax Planning — The process of developing tax-saving and tax-deferral strategies for individuals, trusts, and companies, within the rules of the Income Tax Act of Canada.

Tax Shelter — An investment intended to provide investors with a deferral or reduction of tax.

Tax Smart — Tax effective, or giving consideration to deferring or minimizing tax.

Taxable Capital Gain — The portion of a capital gain that is included in your income for tax purposes. The taxable portion is 75% of the net capital gains.

Taxable Income — The amount of income that is subject to tax after all permitted tax deductions have been made. The relevant tax rate is applied to taxable income.

Tax-Advantaged Income — The opposite of tax-disadvantaged income.

Tax-Deferred Growth — Investment growth that attracts no current taxation. Tax-deferred growth occurs inside tax-sheltered plans like registered pension plans, RRSPs, or RRIFs. Accruing capital gains on investments also grow tax deferred until realized. Tax-deferred growth means that tax will be paid on this investment when it is eventually sold or removed from its tax-sheltered protection.

Tax-Disadvantaged Income — Investment income that is subject to a higher rate of tax than other types of investment income. The opposite of tax-advantaged income.

Interest income and employment income are tax disadvantaged since they generally attract a higher tax rate than dividends and capital gains.

Term Certain Annuity — An annuity that provides a stream of payments to an investor for a fixed period of time; as opposed to a life annuity, which provides payments for the life of the annuitant.

TIPS — See TSE 35 Index Participation units.

Tracking Error — The difference between the performance of an index and the performance of a mutual fund that is attempting to mirror that index, when the fund company doesn't buy and sell the appropriate investments at exactly the same time that the index's components change. Fund returns are also decreased by fees to the fund company to manage the fund and pay the operating costs.

Trailer Fee — A fee paid to an investment advisor by a mutual fund company when one of its funds has been purchased through that advisor. The investment advisor may receive trailer fees as long as the advisor is used by the client to hold his or her investments. The trailer pays for ongoing service provided to the client by the advisor.

Treasury Bill — Short-term debt issued by the federal and some provincial governments at a discount, to mature at face value. There is no interest paid; rather, the difference between the purchase price and maturing value is taxed as interest income.

Trust — See formal trust.

Trustee — The administrator of a trust.

TSE 35 Index Participation Units (TIPS) — These units are created by the Toronto Stock Exchange to permit investors to own a piece of the TSE 35 Index, which consists of some of the largest and most heavily traded publicly listed companies in Canada, and is a subset of the TSE 300. Ownership of the TSE 35 offers diversification geographically and across industries; it offers liquidity, as the units are easy to sell; and it offers the flow-through of dividend payments paid by the companies owned by the units. Most of the 35 companies included in the TIPS index have a market capitalization greater than $1 billion.

TSE 300 Composite Index — A Canadian index of public company stocks representing 300 of the largest companies in Canada trading on the Toronto Stock Exchange. The TSE 300 is widely used as a measure of the performance of the stock market in Canada.

T3 Slip — A federal government form used to report income and capital gains received from owning an interest in a trust (including a mutual fund trust). Income and capital gains reported on a T3 slip should be reported on your personal tax return in the year received.

Undervalued Investment — An investment that is selling for less than it is thought to be worth, based on the company's net assets and performance.

Unit — A measure of ownership of an open-ended mutual fund. Units are bought and sold to reflect ownership in the fund. The unit value fluctuates with the increases and decreases in value of the investments inside the fund.

Unit Holder — An owner of units in a mutual fund.

Universal Life Insurance — A form of permanent life insurance where the insurance component and the savings element are separate and distinct, and the policy owner may have several investment options to consider for the savings part of the policy, along with flexibility on the timing and amount of premium deposits.

Unrealized Gain — The opposite of a realized gain.

Venture Capital — Money used to invest in business ventures. These business ventures, in some cases, may be higher risk opportunities that cannot otherwise obtain money for investment.

Vesting — The right to keep one's benefits that have been created by an employer's contributions to a pension plan. Before contributions are vested, an employee may lose all employer-contributed benefits to his or her pension if he or she leaves the employer. The benefits of vesting also apply to stock options.

Wrapped Investment Account or Product — An investment for which professional money managers have been contracted to manage pieces of the investment portfolio. A wrapped product might consist of mutual funds, pooled funds, or segregated money management. All fees are combined into one that is charged to the investor. Wrapped products thus provide access to multiple money managers through one source.

Yield — The amount of return generated by an investment, expressed as a percentage. Dividend yields for stocks are calculated by dividing the annual dividend by the current market price of the stock. Bond yields factor interest payments together with the difference between purchase price and face value and maturity date.

Kurt Rosentreter, CA, CFP,

Advisor, Author, and Educator

Vice President, Ernst & Young Investment Advisers Inc.

Within a very short period of time, Kurt Rosentreter has established himself as a leading authority on issues of taxation and investment in Canada.

Kurt's business experience has positioned him to be one of Canada's leaders in the field of wealth management. After obtaining his Honours Finance/Investment Management degree at the University of Manitoba, he launched an investment management career within the TD Bank. Shortly thereafter, he moved on to obtain his CA designation in public practice at Ernst & Young LLP — Canada's largest professional services firm. At Ernst & Young LLP, Kurt broadened his wealth management skills to include a specialization in income tax, completion of the Canadian securities course, and achievement of his Certified Financial Planner designation. Currently, Kurt is working towards the Certified Investment Management Analyst designation, offered through the Wharton Business School in Philadelphia.

Kurt was asked to make the move from Winnipeg to Toronto to spearhead the launch of Ernst & Young's LLP national investment counselling practice and wealth management department — a practice that offers tax-effective portfolio design and optimization wrapped up with comprehensive wealth management services. As Vice President of Ernst & Young Investment Advisers Inc., Kurt's services extend to every area of financial planning — a challenging role that sees him responsible for selling services, executing services, and building the practice in his national mandate to create a successful wealth management practice. In just over one year, this practice has grown to approximately $1 billion of client assets under management.

Kurt is actively involved in some of Canada's most influential governing bodies in the area of financial advisory services. He is Director of Membership of the Ontario Association of Financial Planners (Central Ontario Chapter), and an exam setter for the Financial Planning Standards Council of Canada. He is also the Canadian Institute of Chartered Accountants' representative on the Financial Planning Standards Council Education Committee. In these roles, Kurt is committed to setting a higher level of standards for financial planners to protect both the public's interest and those advisors who are truly professionally qualified and experienced.

The release of the first edition of *50 Tax-Smart Investing Strategies*, in 1998, was well received by the media. The book became a Canadian bestseller just four months after its release. *Money Digest* said that "*50 Tax-Smart Investing Strategies* will change the way you think about investing and financial planning." Following the release of his book, Kurt has been in demand as an expert media resource, and as a speaker on tax and investment issues. He regularly conducts workshops for employee groups, executives, and the general public, and is also called on to educate other financial advisors on topics of taxation, investing, and financial planning.

Kurt has appeared on national television and radio on many occasions, is regularly quoted in the nation's newspapers on tax, investment, and financial planning issues, and writes regularly on financial issues important to Canadians.

Kurt Rosentreter may be reached by email (Jo.Chan@ca.eyi.com or KurtRosentreter@hotmail.com), phone (416-943-2102), or mail (PO Box 251, 222 Bay Street, Toronto, M5K 1J7).

- Kurt is available for public-speaking engagements to educate your clients, advisors, support staff, or conference attendees on a variety of tax, investing, and wealth-management topics.

- Kurt is available for half-day or full-day seminars to educate employees, clients, or advisors. As a seminar sponsor you can choose from a wide variety of presentation topics, including Tax-Smart Investing Strategies, Personal Tax Strategies, Building an Investment Portfolio, and Basic Financial Planning Topics.

- If you would like to be added to Kurt's mailing list to receive continuous updates of new tax-smart strategies, new tax-planning opportunities, and other less-common financial techniques, and to receive copies of his articles carried in *The Globe and Mail*, *The Financial Post*, and other media, provide Kurt (addresses above) with your full name and address.

- If there is a topic you would like Kurt to address in a future edition, please contact him with your suggestions.

Additional information on Kurt Rosentreter can be found at the following websites: www.fapages.com and www.globefund.com